THE OXFORD Junior ATLAS

Editorial Adviser

Patrick Wiegand

Oxford University Press

Acknowledgements

The publishers would like to thank the following for permission to reproduce photographs

AA Photo Library: 37 top right; Aerofilms Limited: 13, 30 all;
Bryan & Cherry Alexander Photography: 58 middle, 61 middle;
Austin Brown/Aviation Picture Library: 66 right;
British Petroleum Shipping Ltd (Fotoflite): 67 right;
Chorley & Handford: 7 all, 32 all, 34;
Comstock Photo Library: 54, 58 bottom left, 59 middle, 60 bottom middle, 61 right;
English Heritage Photographic Library: 37 bottom left;
The Environmental Picture Library: 36, 63 left; FLPA: 60 bottom right;
Greg Evans International; 37 top left, 58 bottom middle, 58 bottom right, 59 bottom left;
Robert Harding Picture Library Ltd: 33 top, 33 middle, 60 top right, 62 top;
Holt Studios International: 31 all;
The Hutchison Library: 33 bottom, 62 bottom;
David Keith Jones/Images of Africa Photobank: 59 bottom right;
Mark Mason: 4 top right, 5;
National Remote Sensing Centre (Airphotogroup): 4 top left;
Marilyn O'Brien: 37 bottom right;
Christine Osborne Pictures: 60 bottom left;
Port of Felixstowe: 67 left; Rex Features: 62 middle;
Science Photo Library: 14, 56 middle, 57, 60 top left, 66 left;
Skyscan: 34 right; Still Pictures: 56 bottom;
The Telegraph Colour Library: 59 bottom middle, 60 top middle, 65;
Tropix Photographic Library: 63 right;
United States Atlantic Fleet Submarine Force:, Public Affairs Office 55.

Cover image:
Tom Van Sant / Geosphere Project, Santa Monica, Science Photo Library.

The illustrations are by Chapman Bounford, Hard Lines, Mike Harkins, and Gary Hinks.

The page design is by Adrian Smith.

OXFORD
UNIVERSITY PRESS

Great Clarendon Street, Oxford OX2 6DP

Oxford University Press is a department of the University of Oxford. It furthers the University's objective of excellence in research, scholarship, and education by publishing worldwide in

Oxford New York

Auckland Bangkok Buenos Aires Cape Town Chennai
Dar es Salaam Delhi Hong Kong Istanbul Karachi Kolkata
Kuala Lumpur Madrid Melbourne Mexico City Mumbai Nairobi
São Paulo Shanghai Taipei Tokyo Toronto

Oxford is a registered trade mark of Oxford University Press in the UK and in certain other countries

First published 1996
Reprinted 1996, with corrections 1997,
1998 (twice), with corrections 1999, 2000, 2001 (twice), 2002 (twice)

ISBN 0 19 831793 X (paperback) ISBN 0 19 831834 0 (hardback)

Printed in Italy by G. Canale & C. S.p.A. - Borgaro T.se - Turin

Contents

Atlas information

Round Earth	4
Flat map	5
Scale	6
Settlements	7
Land height	8
Rivers	9

Countries of the World 10–11

The British Isles

Countries	12
Land height and rivers	13
Weather and climate	14–15
Topographic map	16

The United Kingdom

Topographic map	16
Orkney and Shetland Islands	17
Scottish Highlands and Islands	18–19
Northern Ireland	20
Southern Scotland	21
Northern England	22–23
Wales	24
English West Midlands	25
South East England	26–27
South West England	28–29
People and cities	30
Farms and forests	31
Factories and offices	32
Energy	33
Roads and railways	34
Ports and airports	35
Pollution	36
Conservation	37

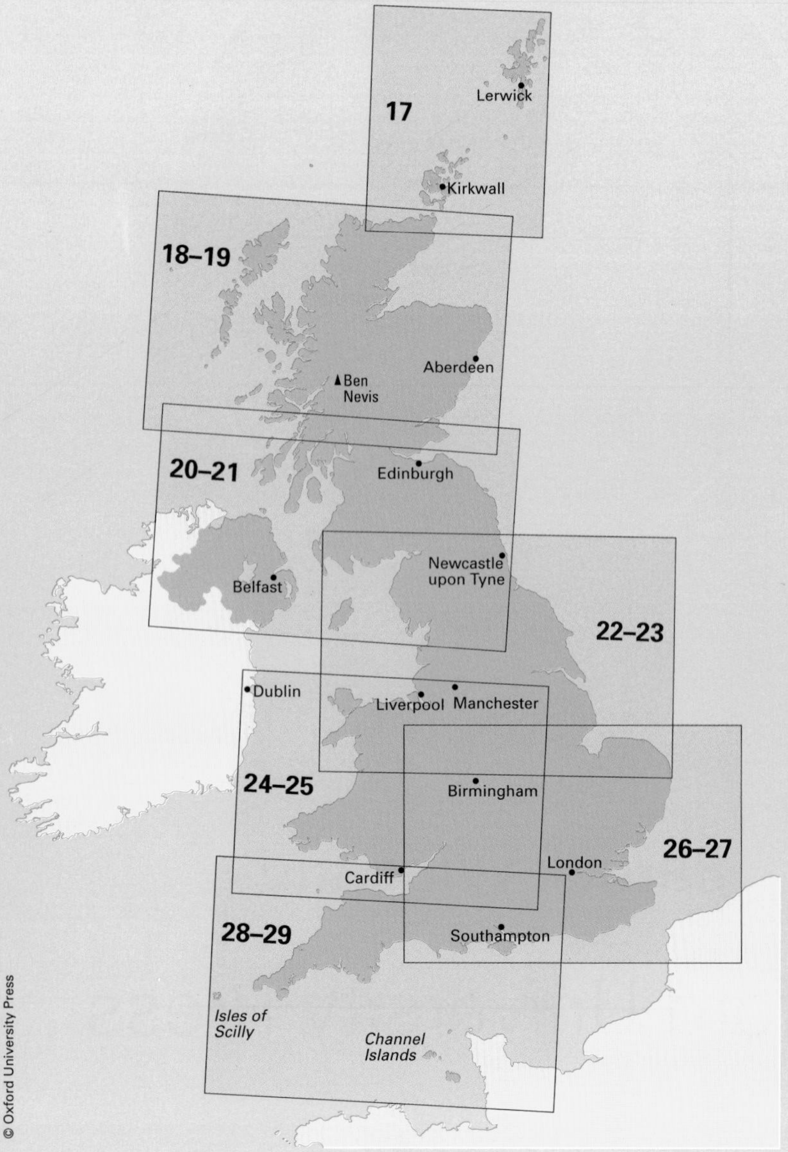
17
Lerwick
Kirkwall
18–19
Ben Nevis
Aberdeen
20–21
Edinburgh
Belfast
Newcastle upon Tyne
22–23
Dublin
Liverpool
Manchester
24–25
Birmingham
London
26–27
Cardiff
28–29
Southampton
Isles of Scilly
Channel Islands

Continents and Poles

Europe	Countries	38–39
	Land height and rivers	40
	Climate	41
Asia	Countries	42–43
	Land height and rivers	44–45
Africa	Countries	46
	Land height and rivers	47
Oceania	Countries	48
	Land height and rivers	49
North America	Countries	50
	Land height and rivers	51
South America	Countries	52
	Land height and rivers	53
Antarctica		54
The Arctic Ocean		55

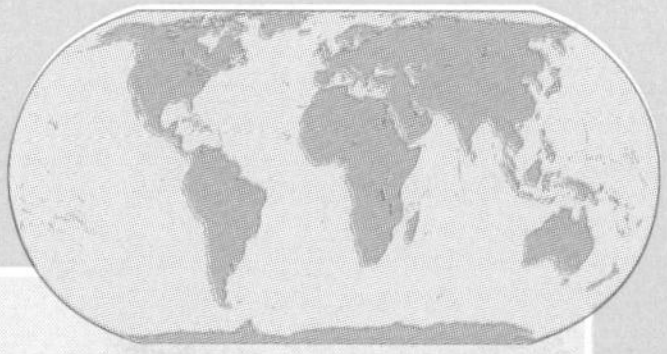

The World

Countries	10–11
Land height and rivers	56–57
Climate	58–59
Environments	60–61
Environmental problems	62–63
People and cities	64–65
Ports and airports	66–67

Liskeard **28** C3
Lismore *island* **18** D1
Lithuania 38 D2
Littlehampton **29** G3
Little Minch *sound* **18** C2
Little Ouse *river* **27** E3

Index

How to use the index	68
Alphabetical list of places	68–72

4 Round Earth

A globe shows the Earth as a sphere.

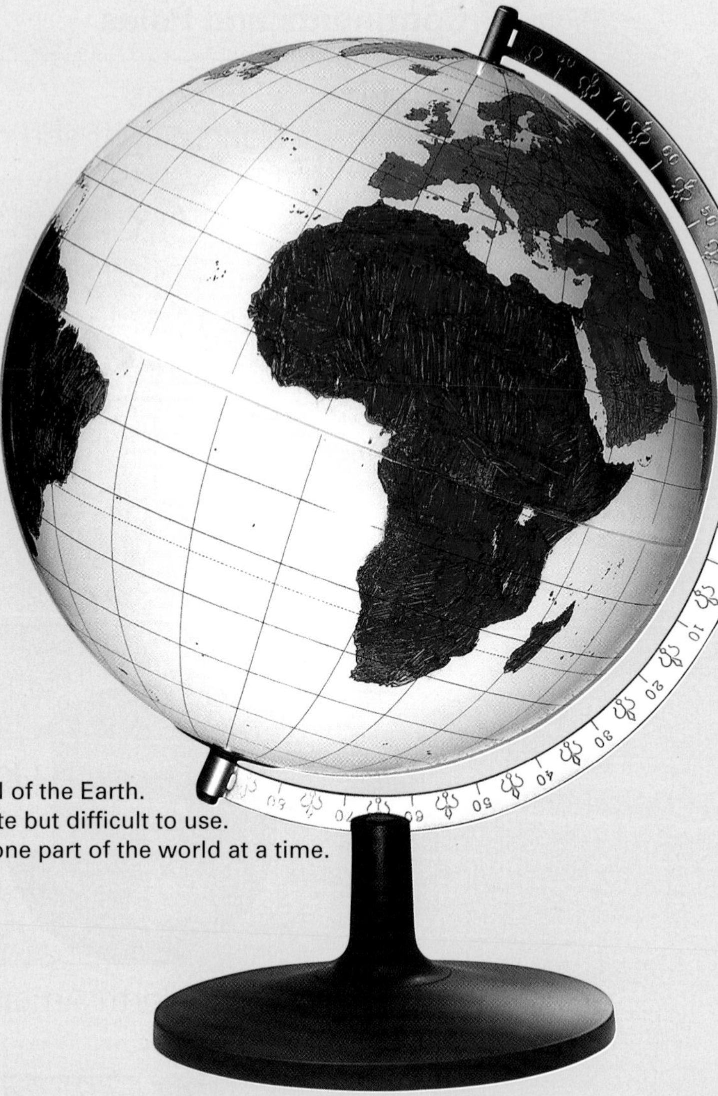

A globe is a model of the Earth.
Globes are accurate but difficult to use.
You can only see one part of the world at a time.

Globes have two sets of lines to help us describe where places are on the Earth.
All the lines are numbered and some have special names.

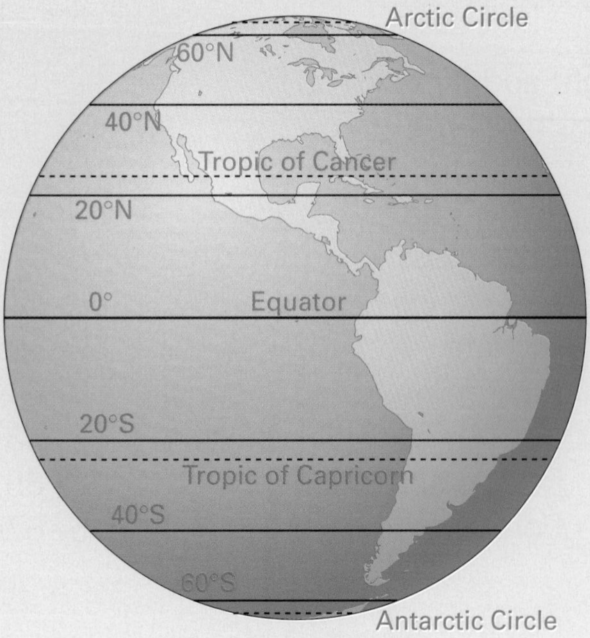

These are lines of latitude.

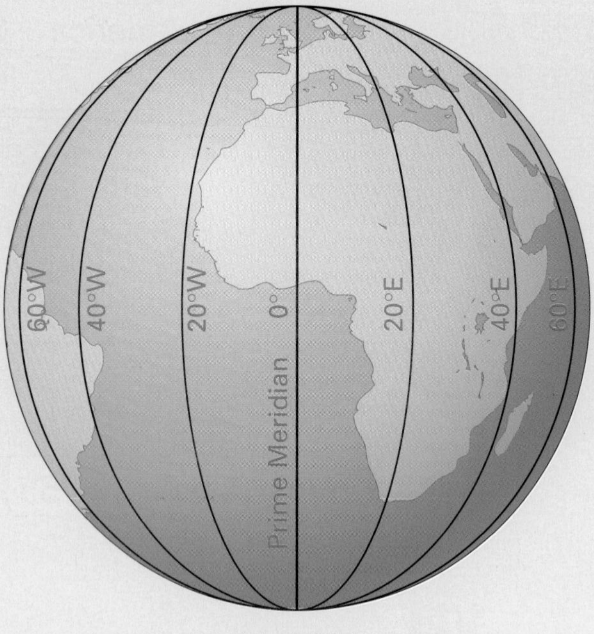

These are lines of longitude.

Flat map

A world map shows the Earth on a flat piece of paper.

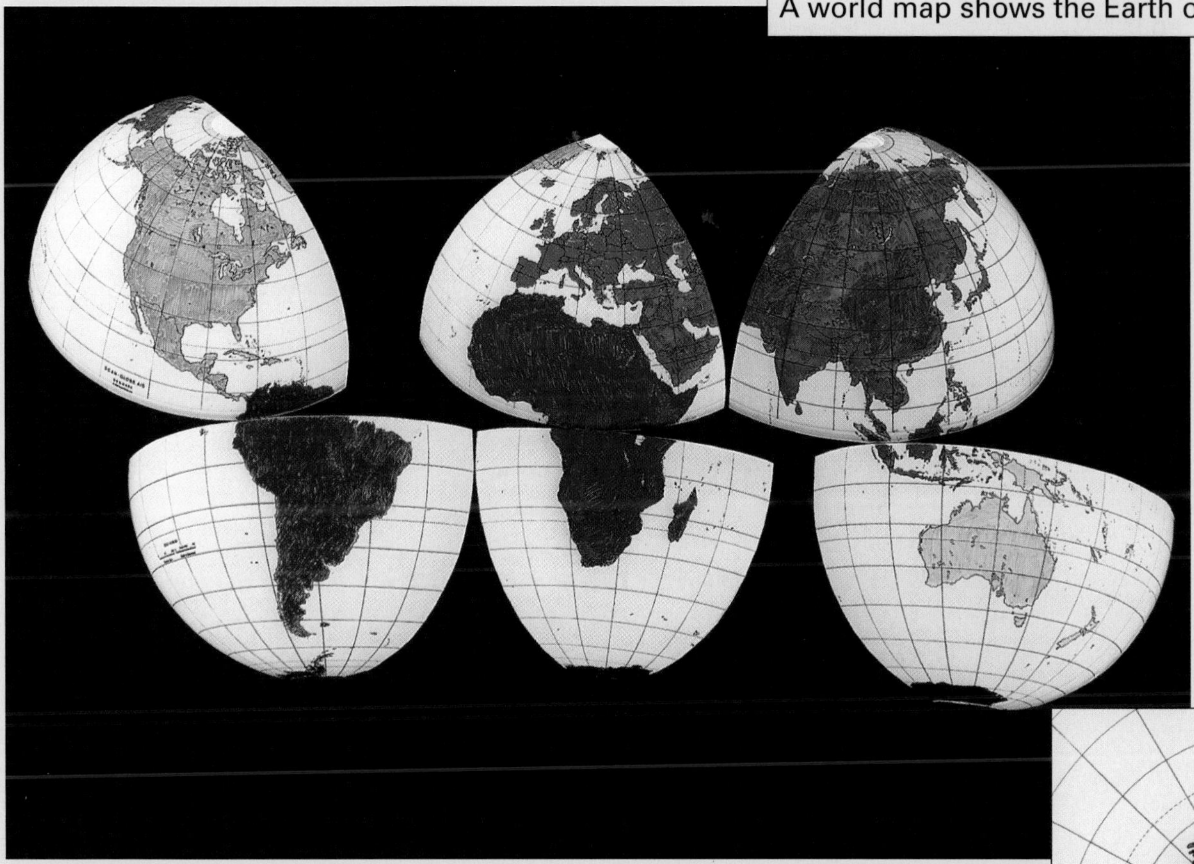

It is difficult to show shapes from a round Earth on a flat map.

Most world maps do not show Antarctica clearly.

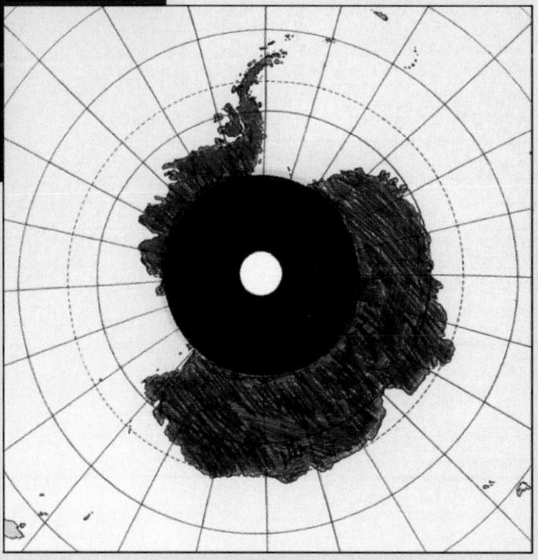

Not all world maps look the same.
There are differences in the shapes and sizes of the continents.
The patterns made by the lines of latitude and longitude are different.
Compare each world map with a globe.

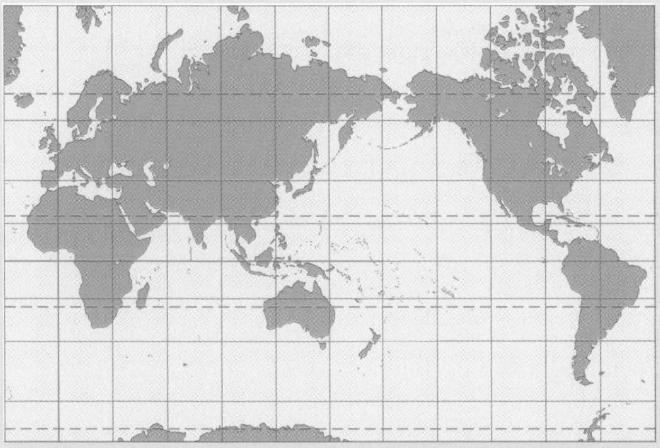

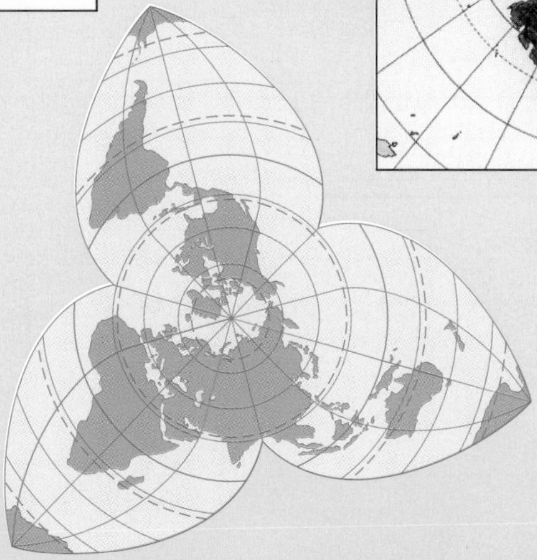

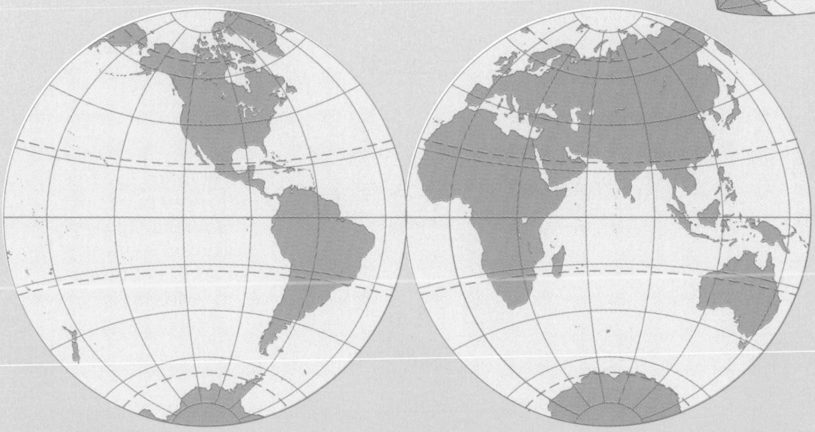

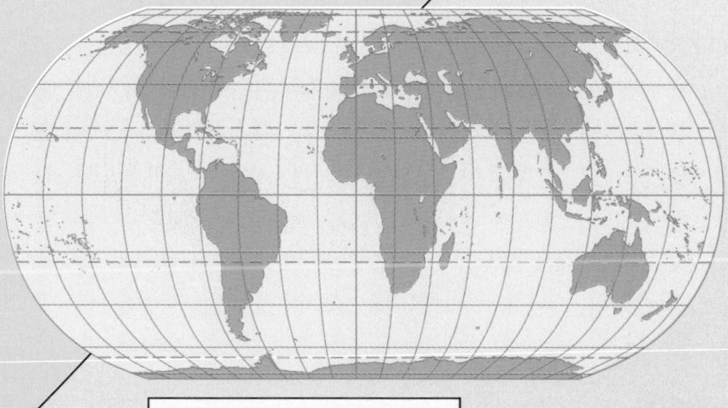

This is the world map used in this atlas.

Scale

Atlas maps have to be much, much smaller than the countries they show.

One centimetre on a map has to stand for many kilometres on the ground.

Every map in this atlas has a sign like this :

12 km
one cm

One centimetre on a map with *this* sign would stand for 12 kilometres on the ground.

You can see more detail on some maps than others. The amount of detail depends on the **scale** of the map.
See how the British Isles become smaller as the scale changes on the maps below.

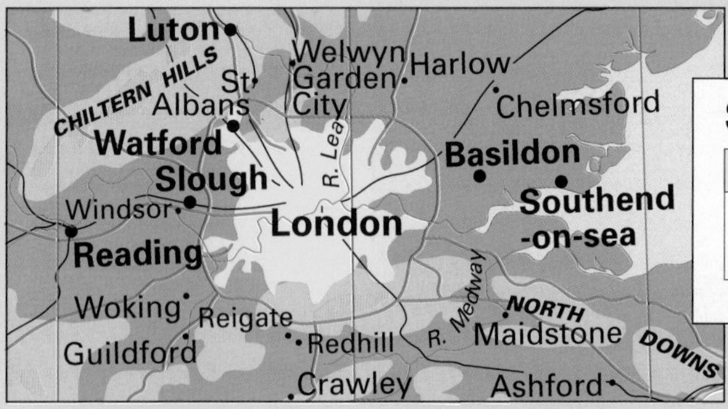

Scale
20 km
one cm

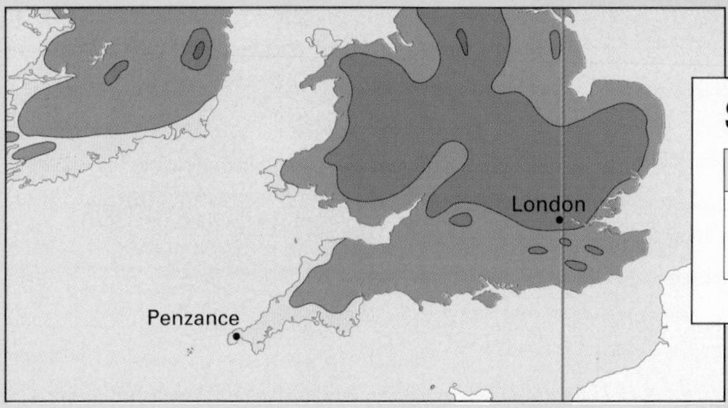

Scale
100 km
one cm

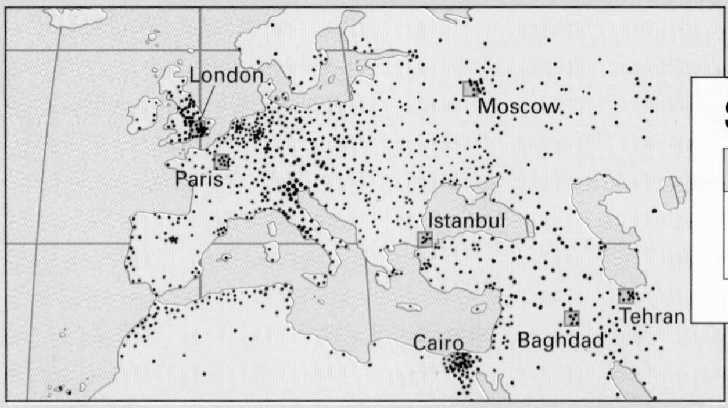

Scale
1000 km
one cm

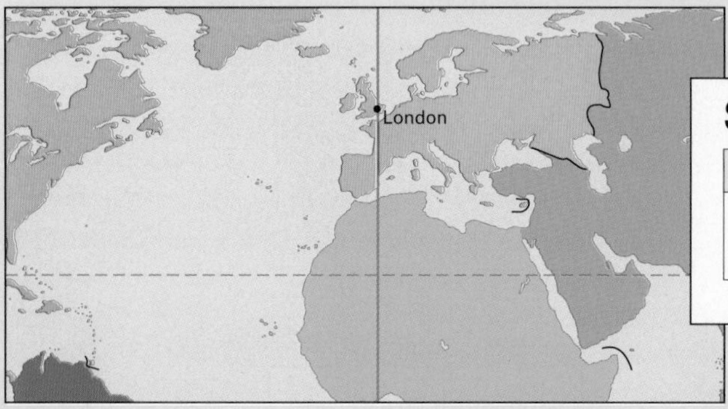

Scale
2000 km
one cm

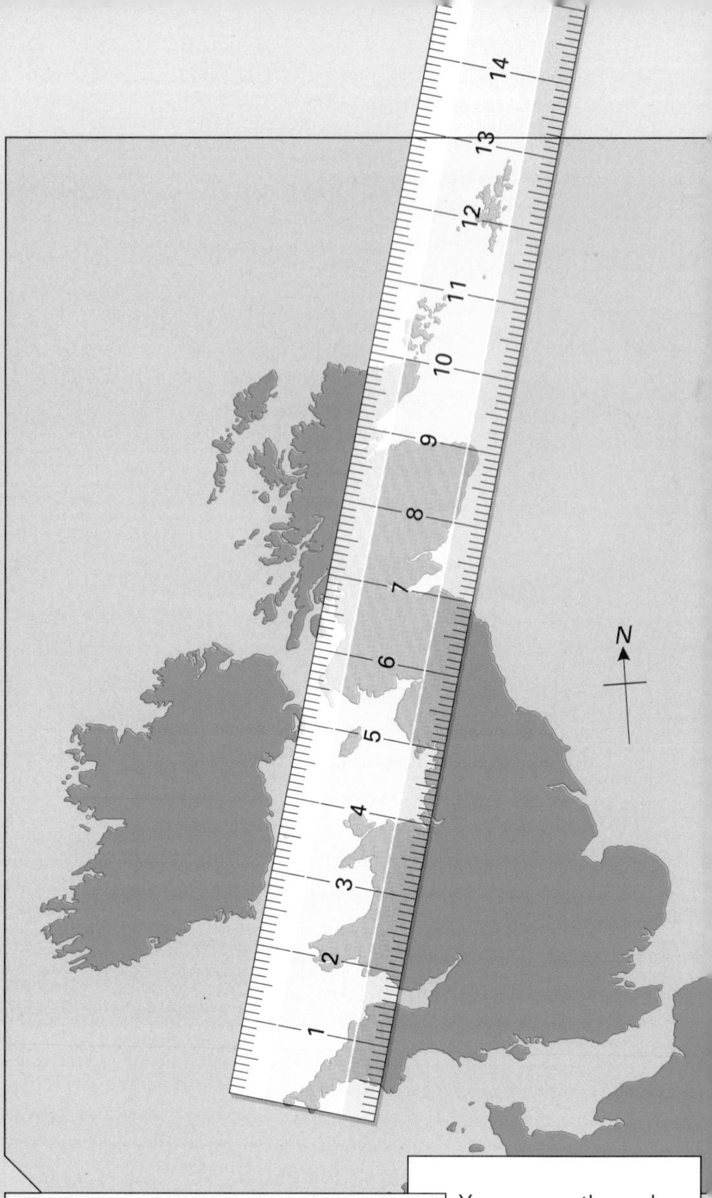

100 km
one cm

One centimetre on the map measures 100 kilometres on the ground.

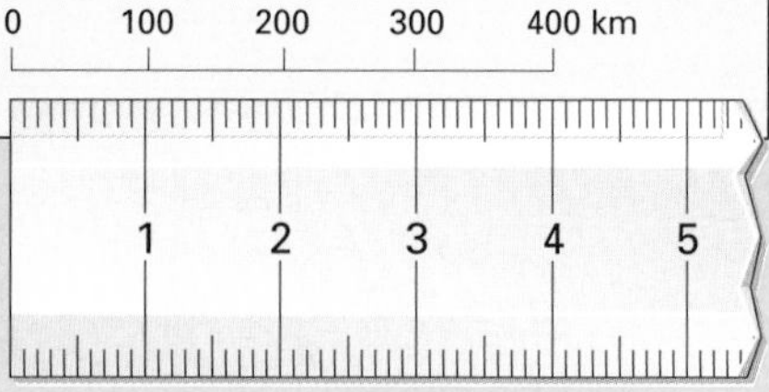

You can use the scale information to measure distances on maps. Great Britain is approximately 1000 km from north to south. Check it with your ruler.

Small maps like this on some pages of the atlas help you to compare the size of other countries with the British Isles.

People live in settlements of different sizes.

Most people in Britain live in towns.
Some towns are large, others are small.
In many parts of the country several towns have grown so large that they have joined to form one huge built-up area.

Each size of settlement has its own map symbol and style of lettering for the place name. Only the largest settlements are marked on atlas maps.

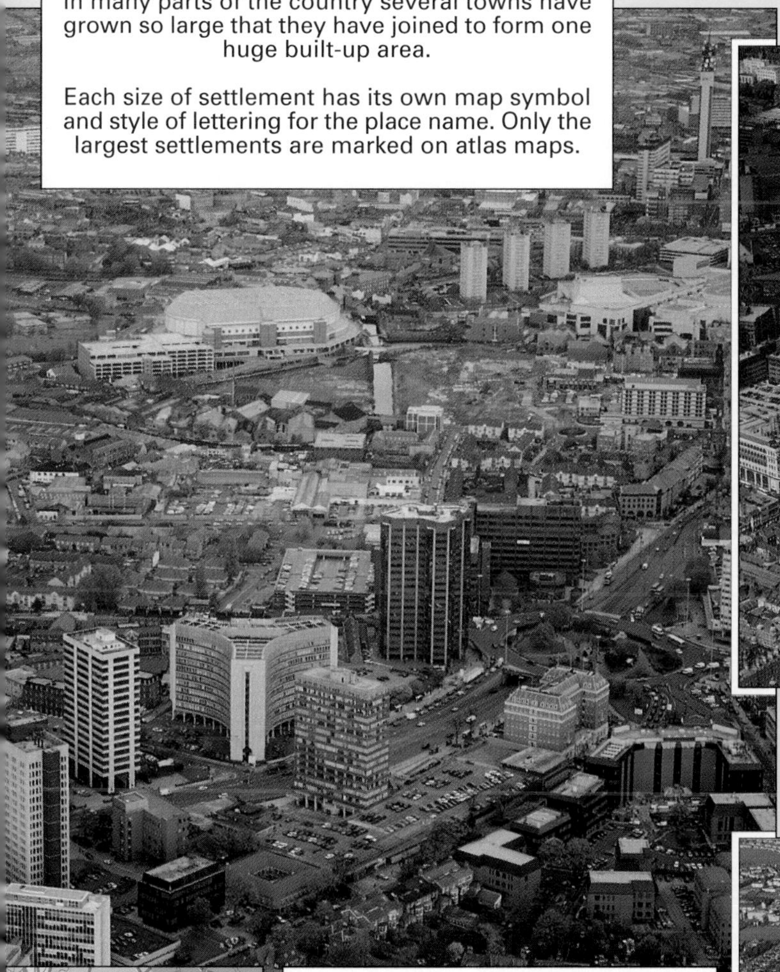

Largest built-up areas
more than 1 million people

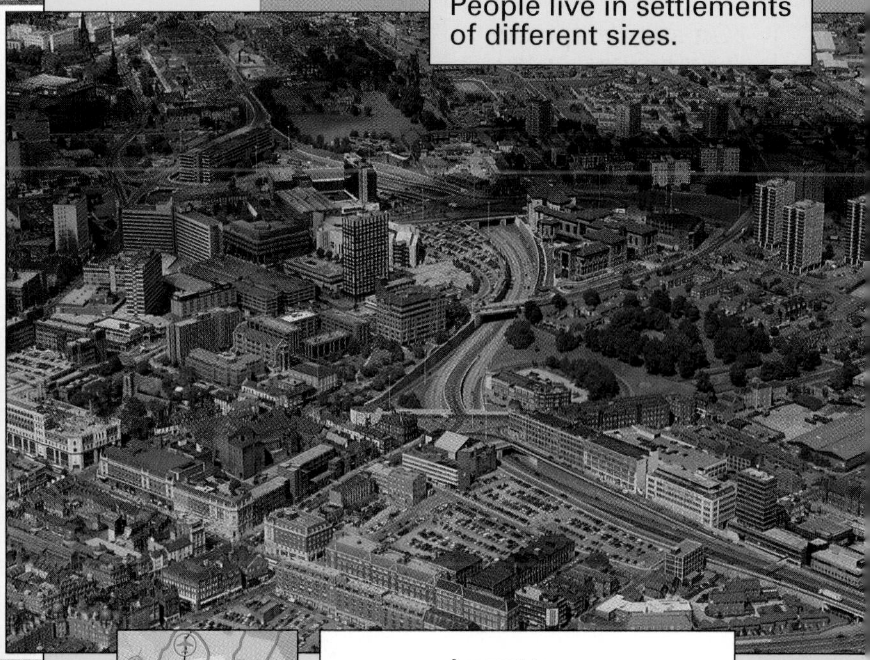

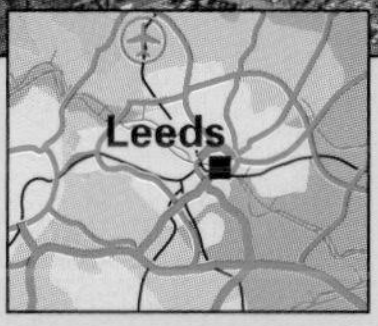

Largest towns
100 000 - 1 million people

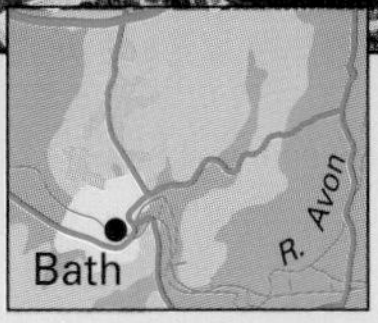

Large towns
25 000 - 100 000 people

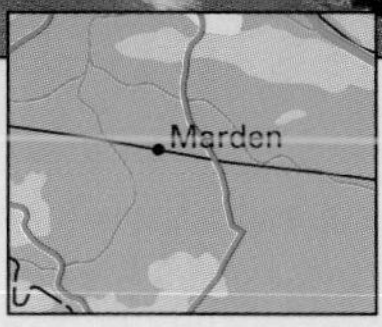

Small towns
10 000 - 25 000 people

Small towns and villages
fewer than 10 000 people

Many very small towns and villages are not shown on atlas maps.

Land Height

On atlas maps the height of the land above sea level is shown by colours.

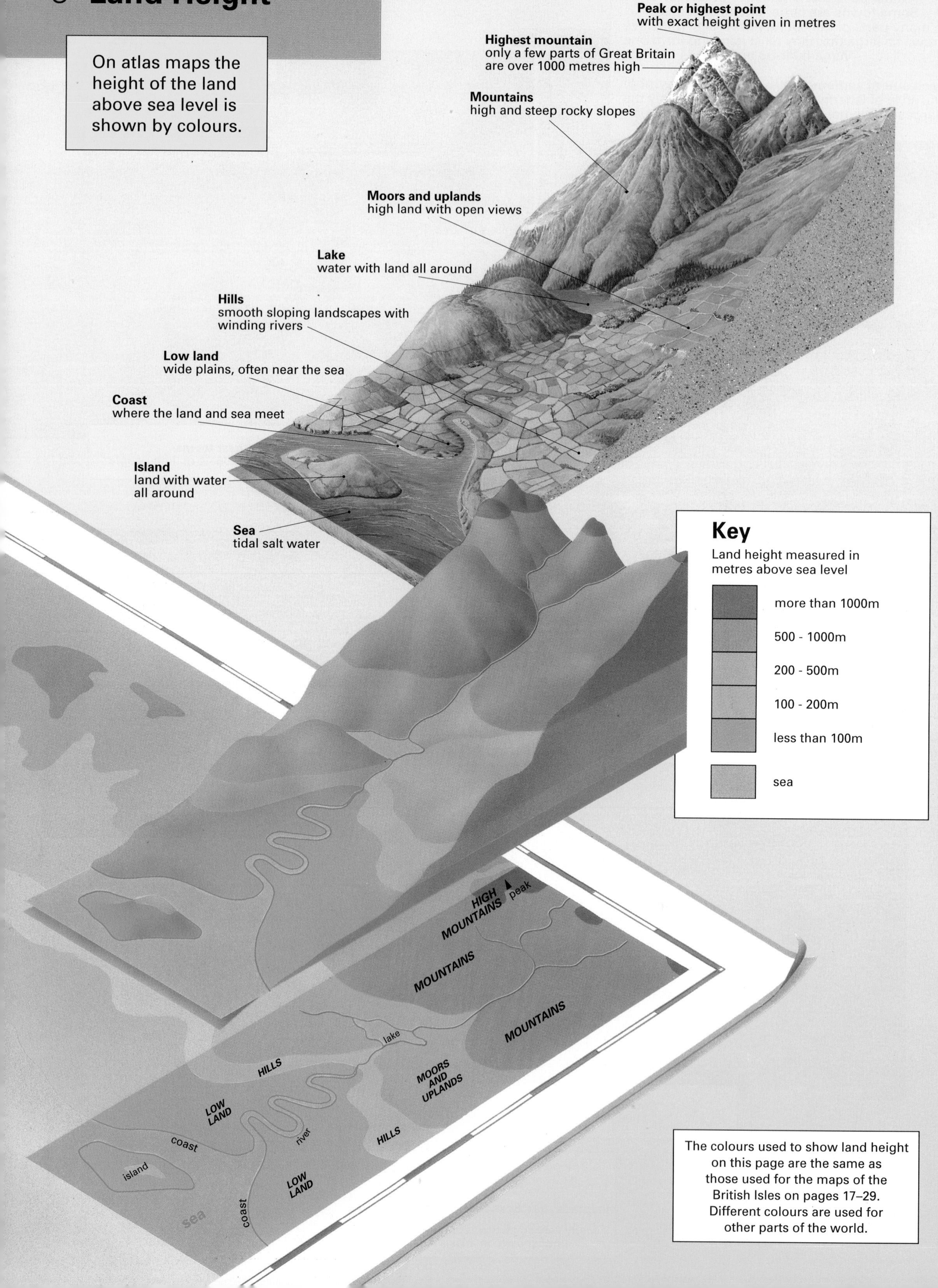

The colours used to show land height on this page are the same as those used for the maps of the British Isles on pages 17–29. Different colours are used for other parts of the world.

Most landscapes in Great Britain have been shaped by rivers.

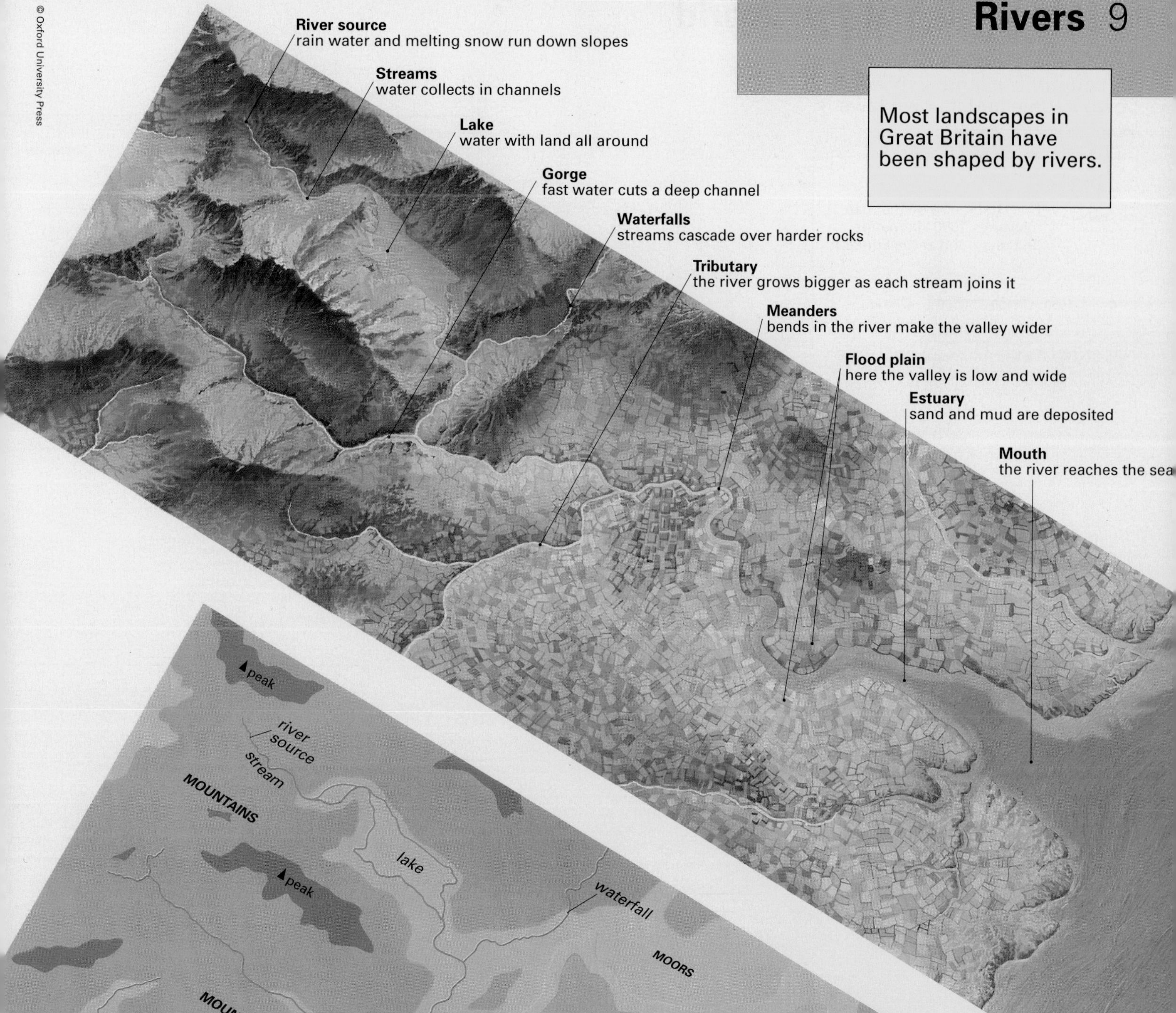

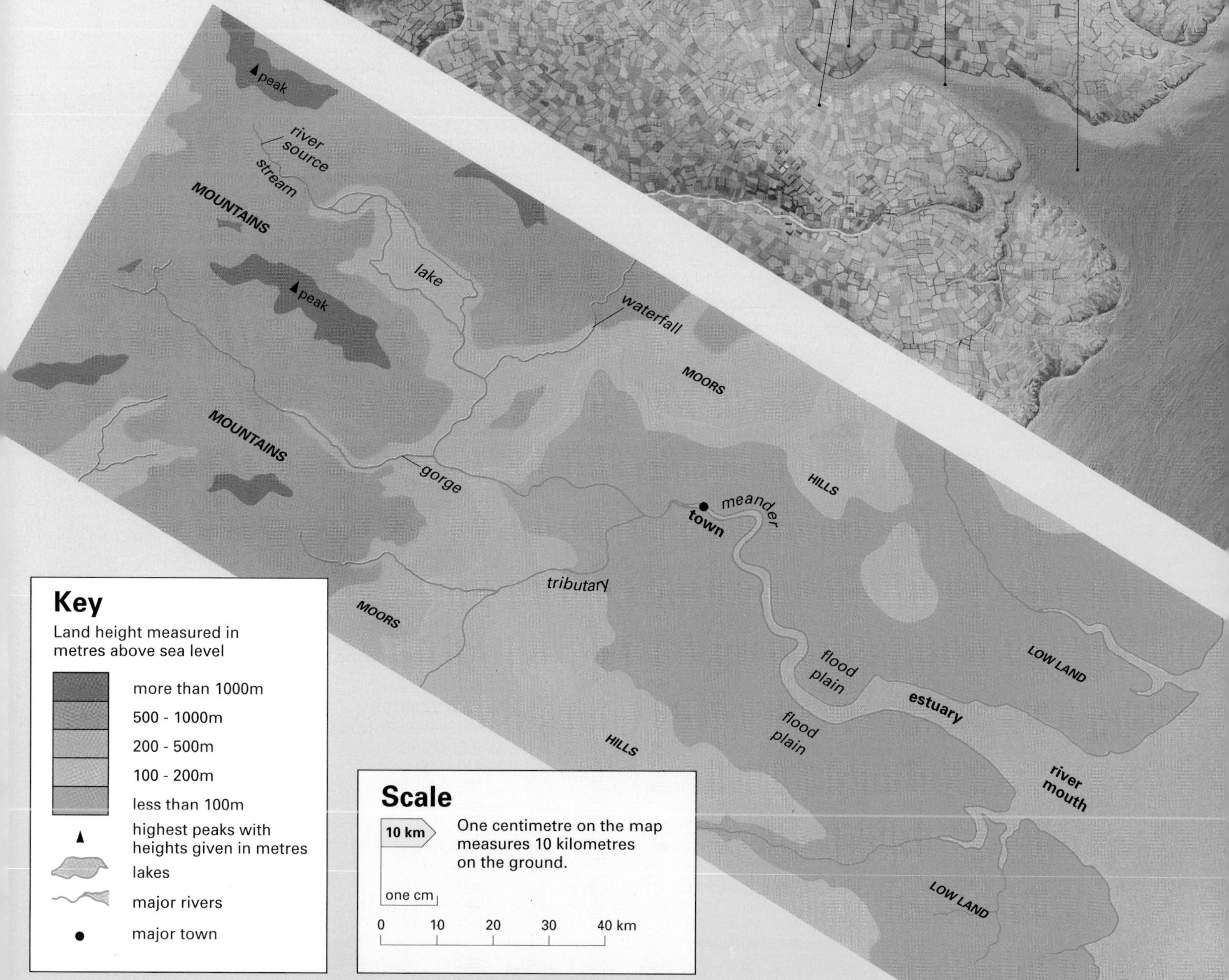

Key

Land height measured in metres above sea level

- more than 1000m
- 500 - 1000m
- 200 - 500m
- 100 - 200m
- less than 100m
- ▲ highest peaks with heights given in metres
- lakes
- major rivers
- ● major town

Scale

10 km — One centimetre on the map measures 10 kilometres on the ground.

one cm

0 10 20 30 40 km

Countries of the World

A country is a land with its own people and its own laws.

Scale

1050 km

One centimetre on the map measures 1050 kilometres on the ground at the Equator.

one cm

0 1050 2100 3150 4200 km

The Continents

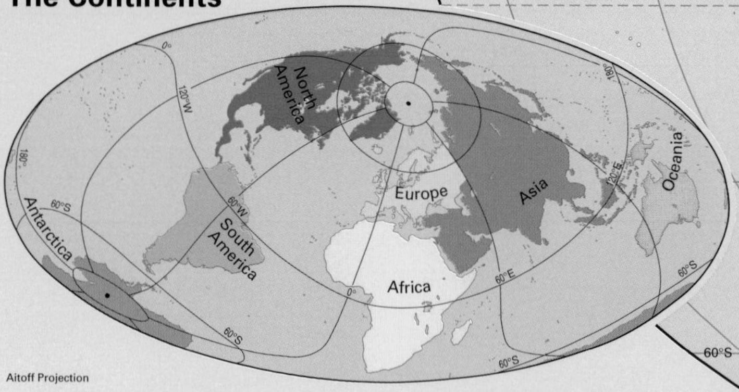

Aitoff Projection

Key

CANADA The names of countries are shown with this type of lettering.

Countries that are too small to be named on the map are shown by the first few letters of their name.

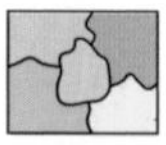

These colours are used to show where one country ends and another begins.

A	ALBANIA	CZ	CZECH REPUBLIC	N	NETHERLANDS
AR	ARMENIA	F	FYROM (FORMER YUGOSLAV REPUBLIC OF MACEDONIA)	Q	QATAR
AU	AUSTRIA			R	ROMANIA
AZ	AZERBAIJAN			S	SLOVAKIA
B	BELGIUM	G	THE GAMBIA	SL	SLOVENIA
BD	BRUNEI DARUSSALAM	G-B	GUINEA-BISSAU	SW	SWITZERLAND
BE	BENIN	H	HUNGARY	T	TAJIKISTAN
BH	BOSNIA-HERZEGOVINA	IS	ISRAEL	TU	TURKMENISTAN
BU	BURKINA	L	LEBANON	U	UGANDA
C	CROATIA	LI	LITHUANIA	UAE	UNITED ARAB EMIRATES
CAR	CENTRAL AFRICAN REPUBLIC	LU	LUXEMBOURG	Y	YUGOSLAVIA
				ZIM	ZIMBABWE

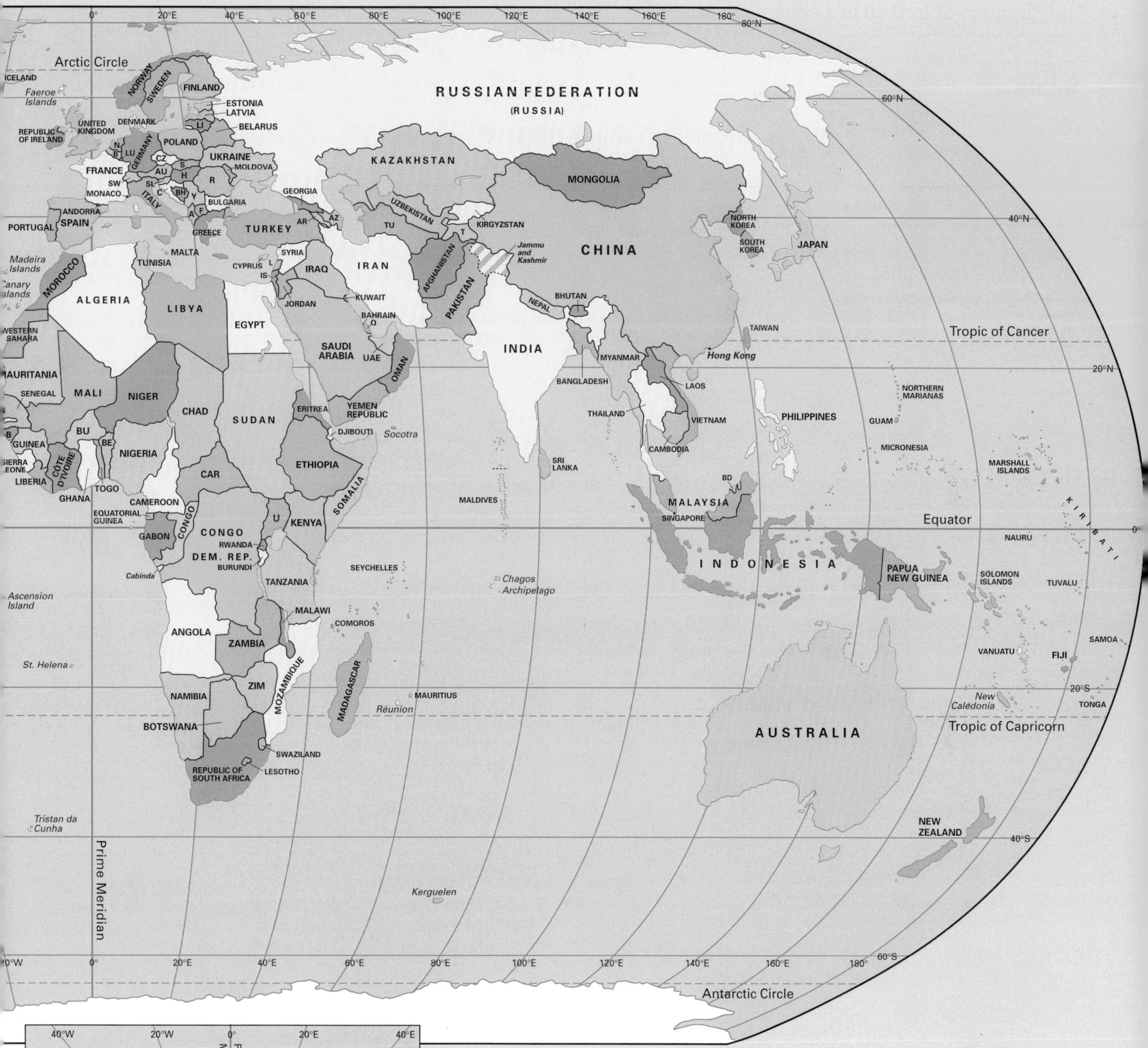

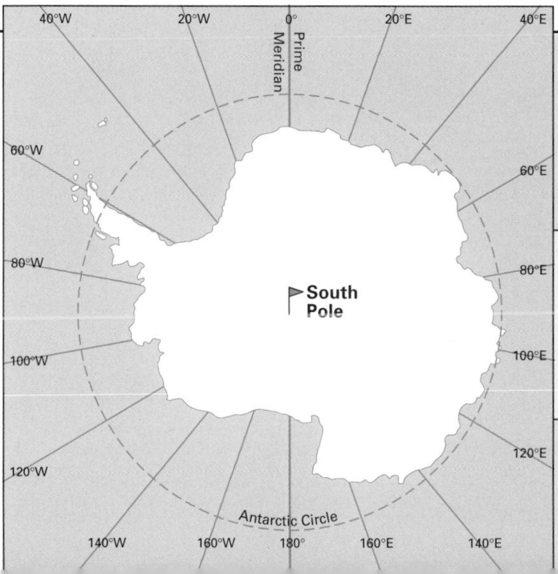

There are no countries in Antarctica. Scientists from all over the world live and work there in research stations.

There are more than 200 countries in the world. The exact number is always changing. Sometimes countries break up into separate states and others join up to make new countries.

Eckert IV Projection

The British Isles Countries

England, Scotland, and Wales, together with Northern Ireland, form the United Kingdom. The Republic of Ireland is a separate country.

Scale

45 km

One centimetre on the map measures 45 kilometres on the ground

one cm

0 45 90 135 180 km

England is divided into counties and some new unitary authorities. Wales and Scotland are divided into unitary authorities. Northern Ireland is divided into districts.

The Republic of Ireland is divided into counties.

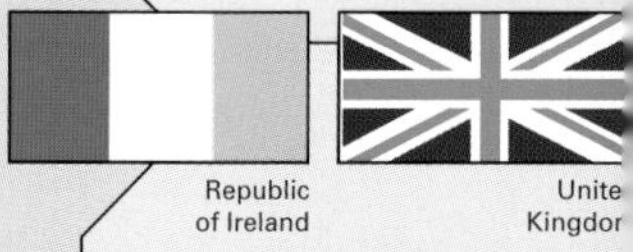

The British Isles consists of the two large islands of Great Britain and Ireland and a number of smaller islands.

Key to unitary authorities in Scotland

1 West Dunbartonshire
2 East Dunbartonshire
3 North Lanarkshire
4 Glasgow City
5 East Renfrewshire
6 Renfrewshire
7 Inverclyde
8 Clackmannanshire
9 Falkirk
10 West Lothian
11 City of Edinburgh
12 Midlothian
13 East Lothian
14 North Ayrshire
15 East Ayrshire
16 Dundee City

Key to districts in Northern Ireland

1 Belfast
2 Newtownabbey
3 Carrickfergus
4 Castlereagh
5 North Down
6 Ards
7 Down
8 Newry & Mourne
9 Banbridge
10 Lisburn
11 Craigavon
12 Armagh
13 Dungannon
14 Fermanagh
15 Omagh
16 Cookstown
17 Magherafelt
18 Strabane
19 Londonderry
20 Limavady
21 Coleraine
22 Ballymoney
23 Moyle
24 Ballymena
25 Larne
26 Antrim

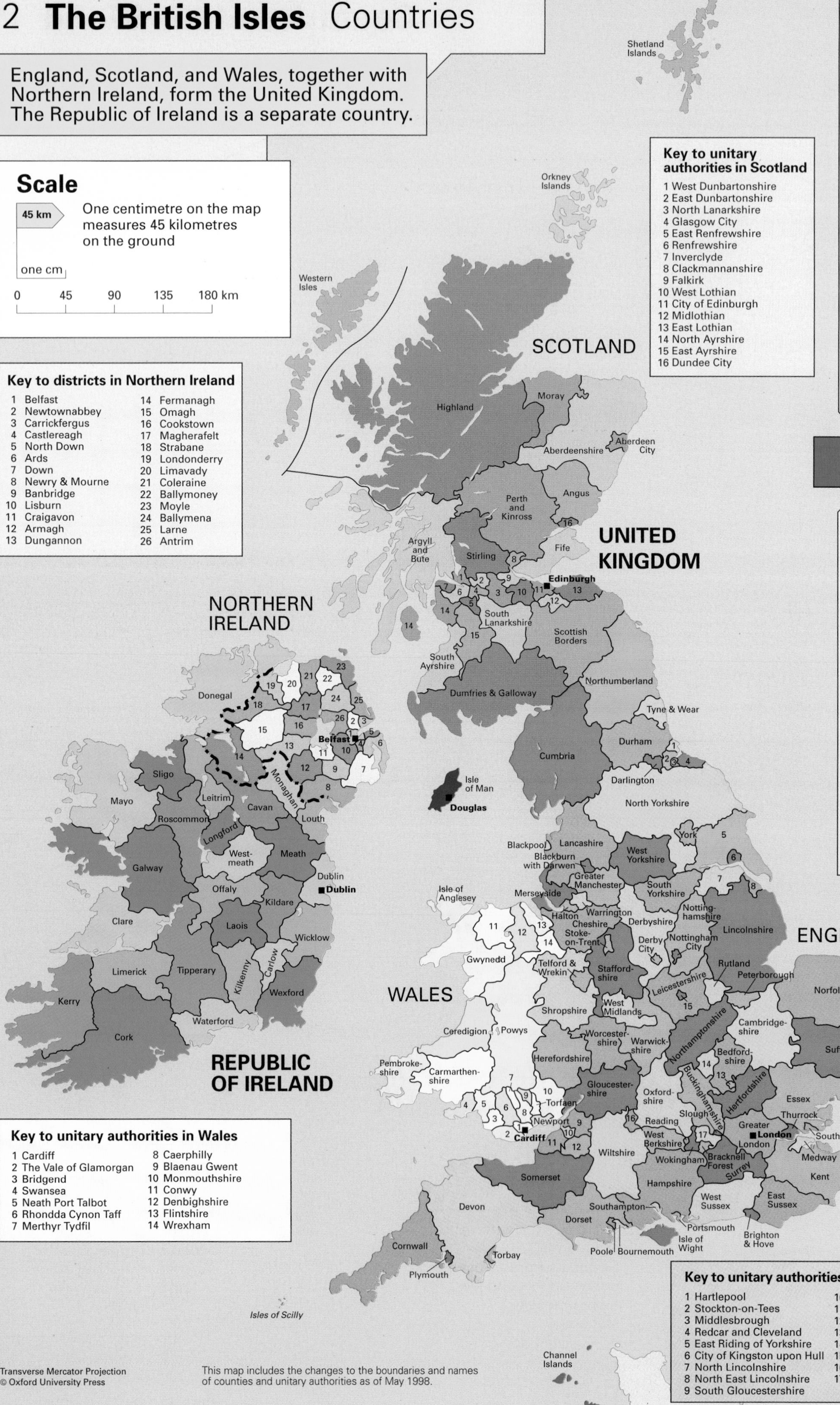

Key to unitary authorities in Wales

1 Cardiff
2 The Vale of Glamorgan
3 Bridgend
4 Swansea
5 Neath Port Talbot
6 Rhondda Cynon Taff
7 Merthyr Tydfil
8 Caerphilly
9 Blaenau Gwent
10 Monmouthshire
11 Conwy
12 Denbighshire
13 Flintshire
14 Wrexham

Key to unitary authorities in England

1 Hartlepool
2 Stockton-on-Tees
3 Middlesbrough
4 Redcar and Cleveland
5 East Riding of Yorkshire
6 City of Kingston upon Hull
7 North Lincolnshire
8 North East Lincolnshire
9 South Gloucestershire
10 Bristol
11 North Somerset
12 Bath and North East Somerset
13 Luton
14 Milton Keynes
15 Leicester City
16 Swindon
17 Windsor & Maidenhead

Transverse Mercator Projection

This map includes the changes to the boundaries and names of counties and unitary authorities as of May 1998.

The British Isles Land height and rivers

The highest parts of Great Britain are mostly in the north and west.

Key

Land height measured in metres above sea level

- more than 1000m
- 500 - 1000m
- 200 - 500m
- 100 - 200m
- less than 100m
- ▲ highest peaks with heights given in metres
- lakes
- major rivers

Scale

45 km — one cm

One centimetre on the map measures 45 kilometres on the ground.

0 45 90 135 180 km

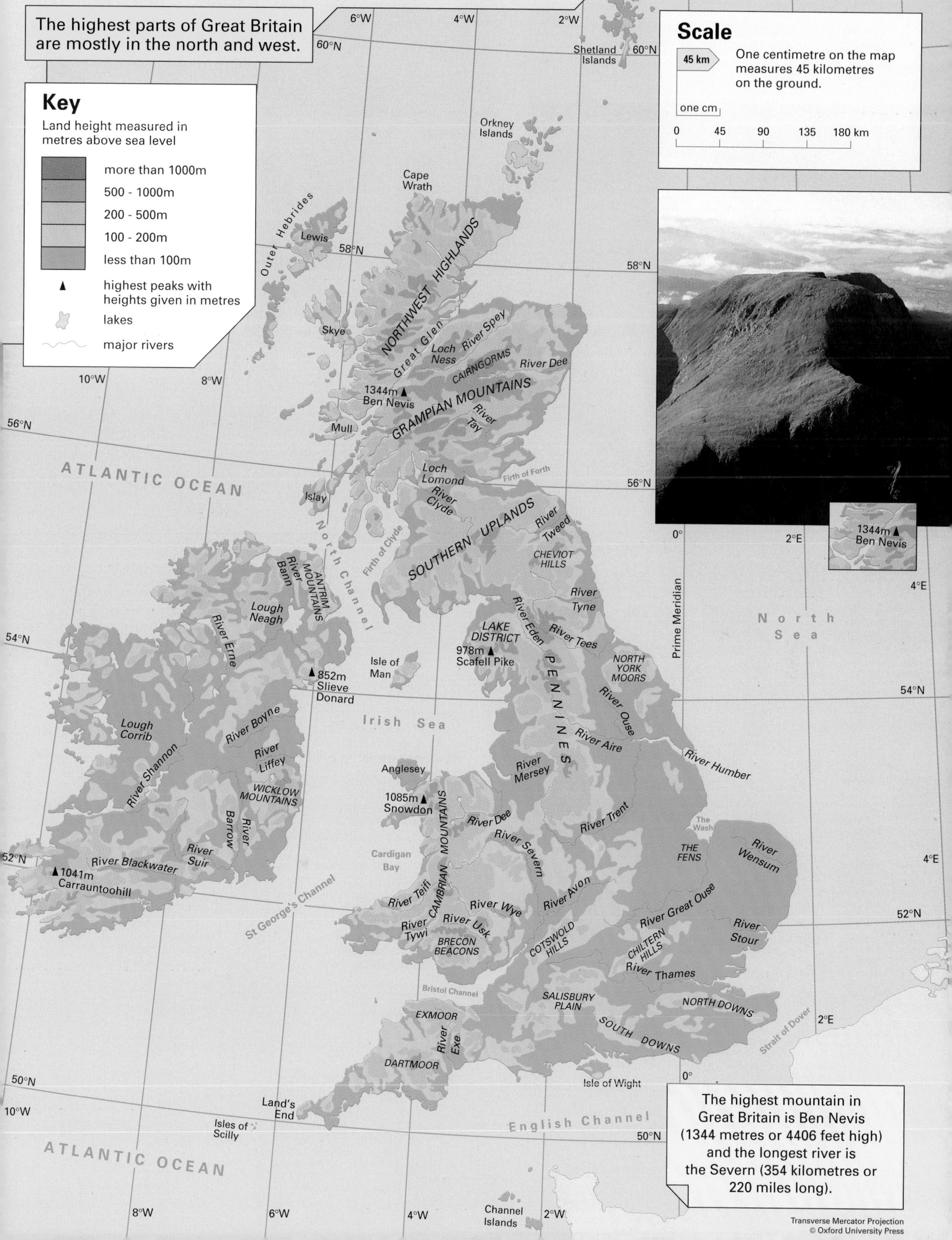

The highest mountain in Great Britain is Ben Nevis (1344 metres or 4406 feet high) and the longest river is the Severn (354 kilometres or 220 miles long).

Transverse Mercator Projection

The British Isles Weather and climate

Climate describes the average pattern of weather over a number of years.

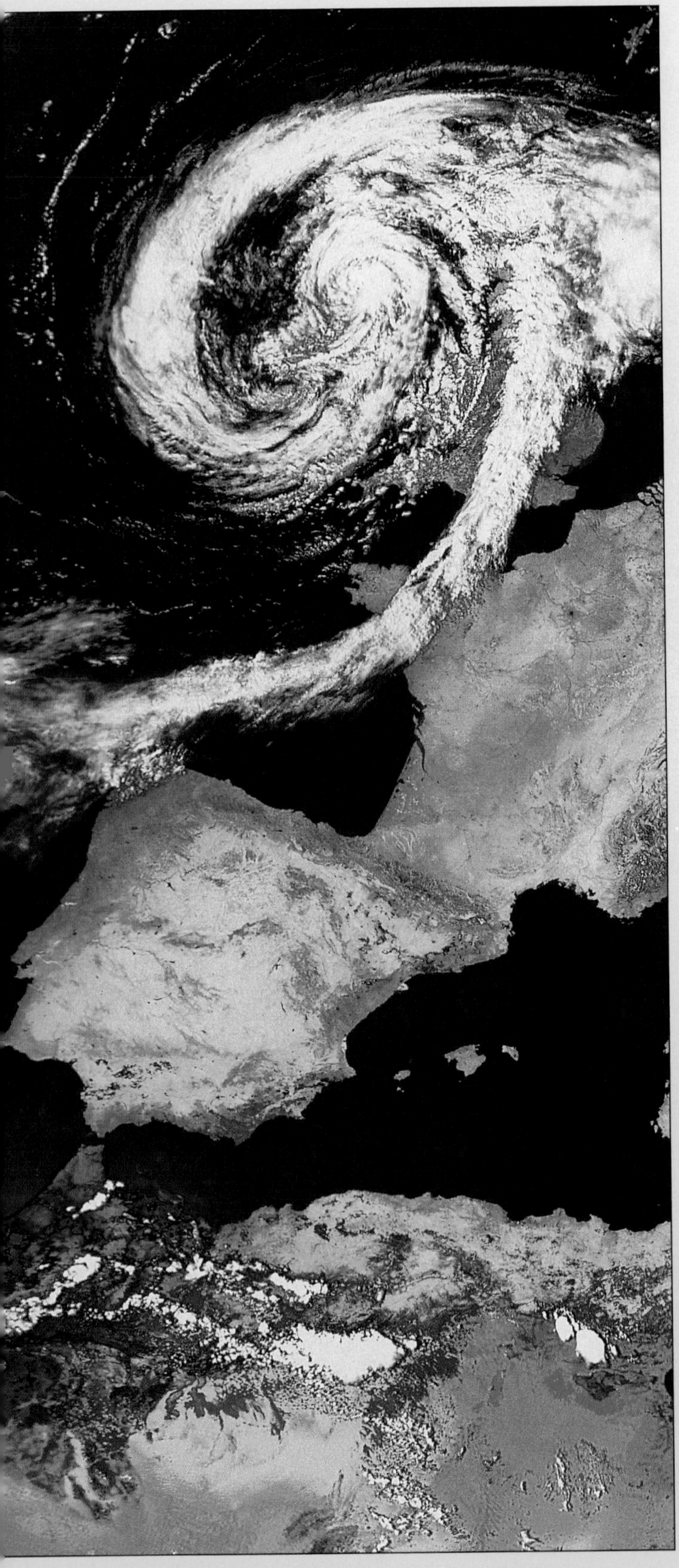

During the year many wet weather bands pass over the British Isles whilst southern Europe stays dry and warm. This is a satellite picture of the weather in western Europe on 6 August 1987.
Satellite pictures like this use colours that are different from the way the land looks to us.

Transverse Mercator Projection

Rainfall

The eastern parts of the British Isles are drier than the western parts. Mountains are wetter than lowlands.

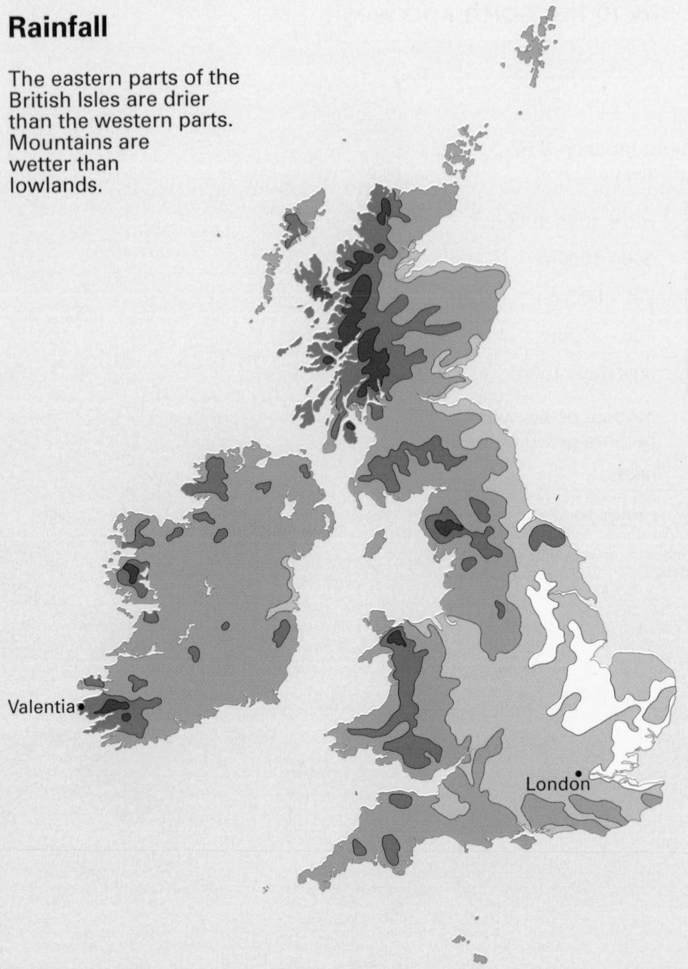

Average annual rainfall in millimetres

(darkest)	over 2400	very wet
	1500 - 2400	quite wet
	800 - 1500	wet
	600 - 800	quite dry
(white)	less than 600	very dry

Average annual rainfall

The graphs show the amount of rainfall in Valentia and London for one year. Valentia is wetter in winter. London has about the same amount of rainfall each month.

All the rain that falls in one year is the **annual rainfall.** Valentia has much more rain than London over the whole year.

Some years are wetter than others. The map shows the amount of rainfall you would expect in an average year.

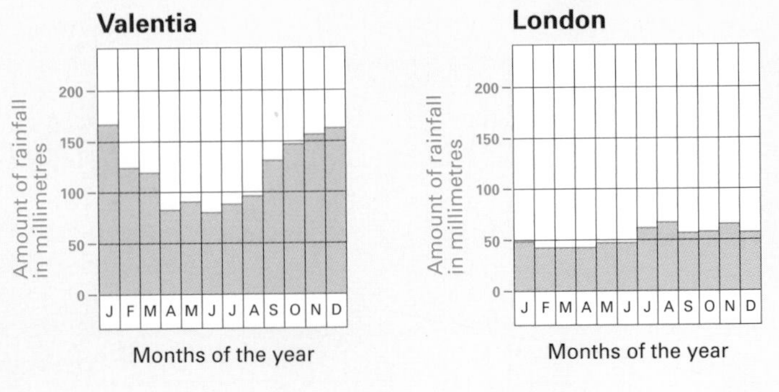

January temperatures

In winter the mountains of Scotland are the coldest parts of the British Isles.

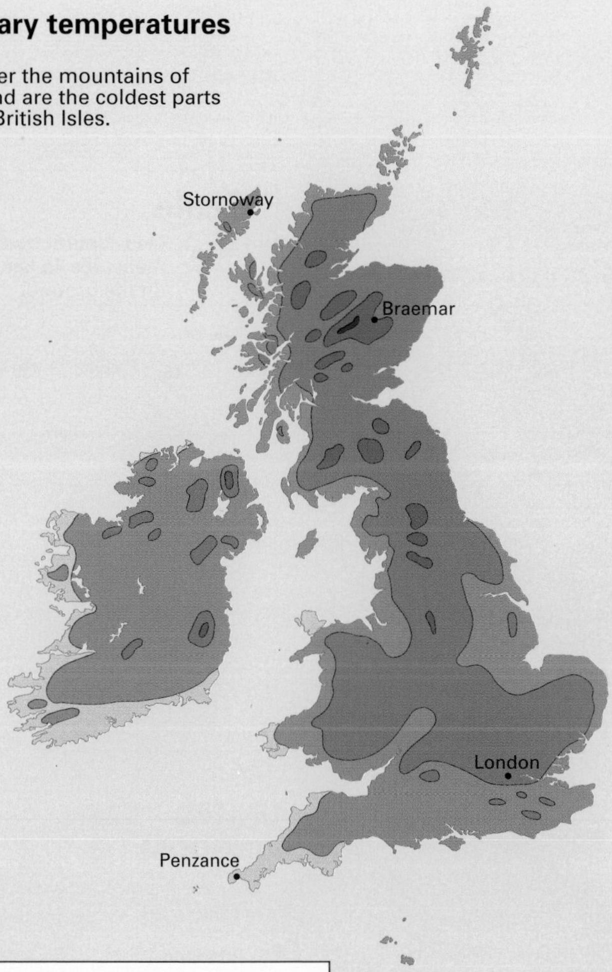

July temperatures

In summer the coasts of southern England are the warmest parts of the British Isles.

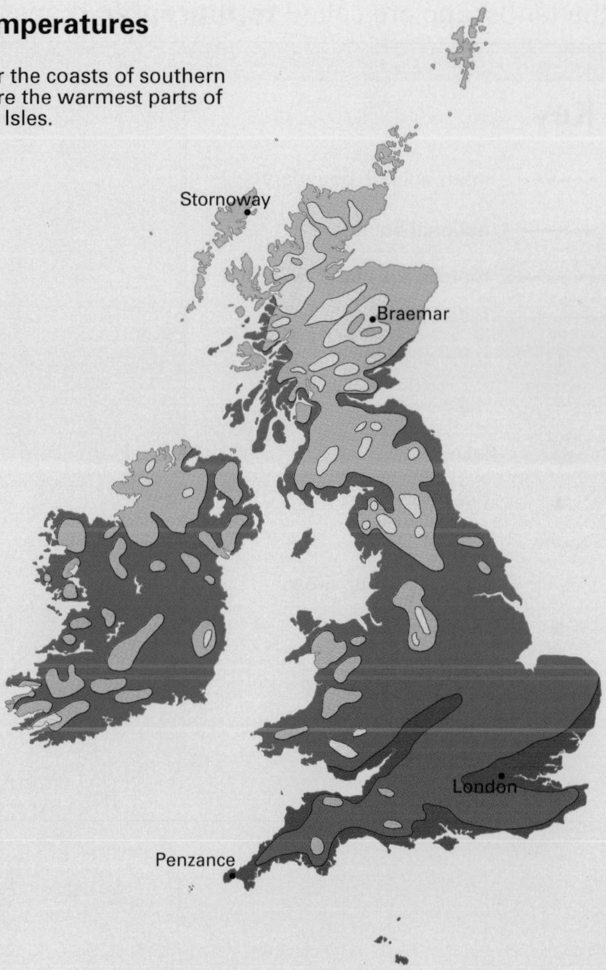

Scale

100 km

One centimetre on the map measures 100 kilometres on the ground.

one cm

Average temperatures in °Celsius

above 16	hot
14 - 16	very warm
12 - 14	warm
10 - 12	quite warm
8 - 10	quite cool
6 - 8	cool
4 - 6	quite cold
2 - 4	cold
0 - 2	very cold
below 0	freezing

In the British Isles it is usually colder in January than in July. However, some years might be very cold whilst others are quite warm. The maps show the temperatures you would expect in an average year.

Average temperatures in winter and summer

The graphs show the average temperatures each month for Stornoway, Braemar, London, and Penzance. In all four places it is warmer in summer than in winter.

Summers in Stornoway and Braemar are much cooler than in London or Penzance. Winter in Braemar is very cold.

Stornoway

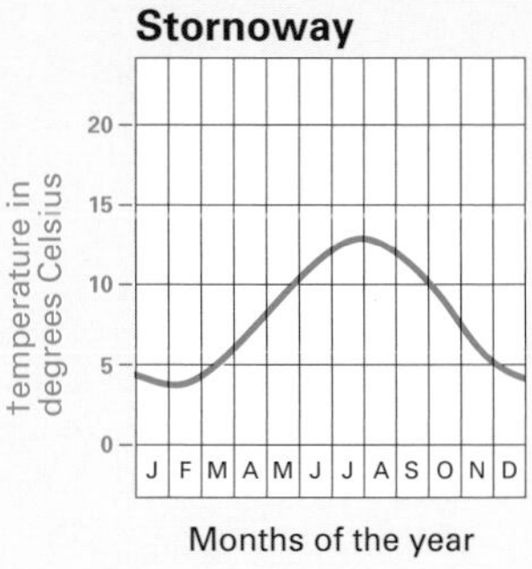

Braemar

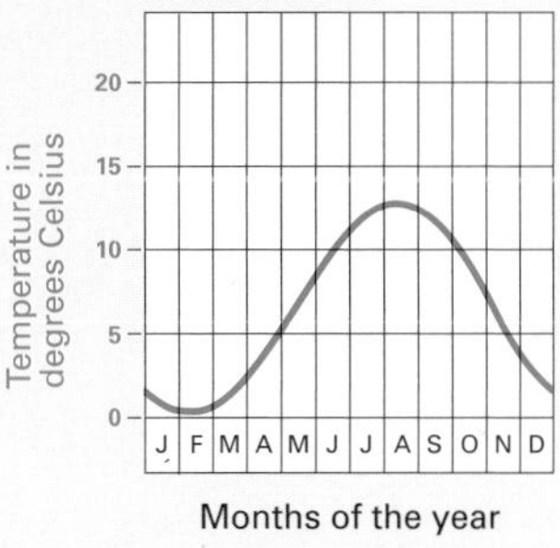

London

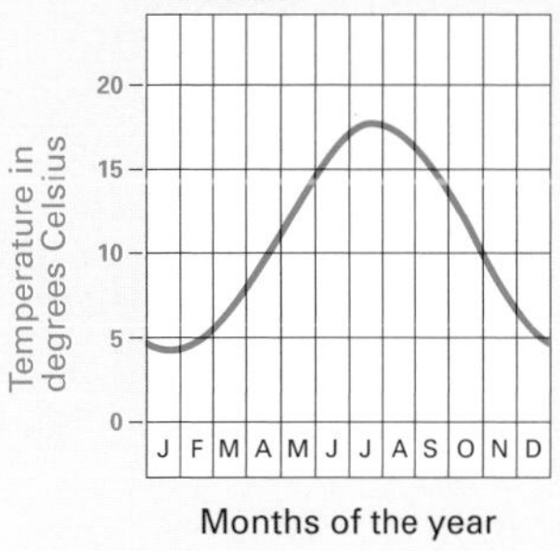

Penzance

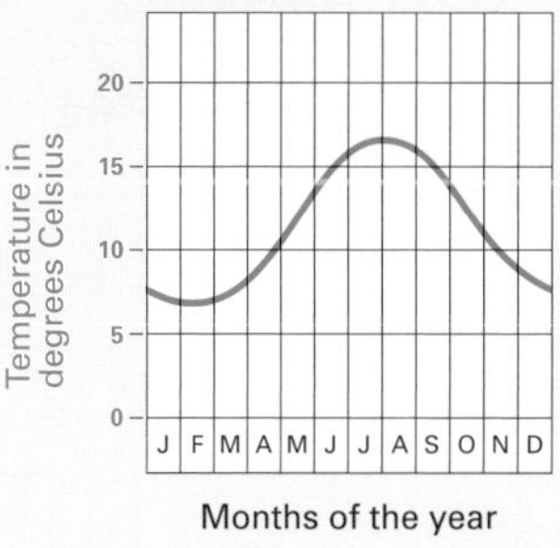

16 **The British Isles** Topographic map

Maps that show all the most important features of the landscape are called **topographic** maps.

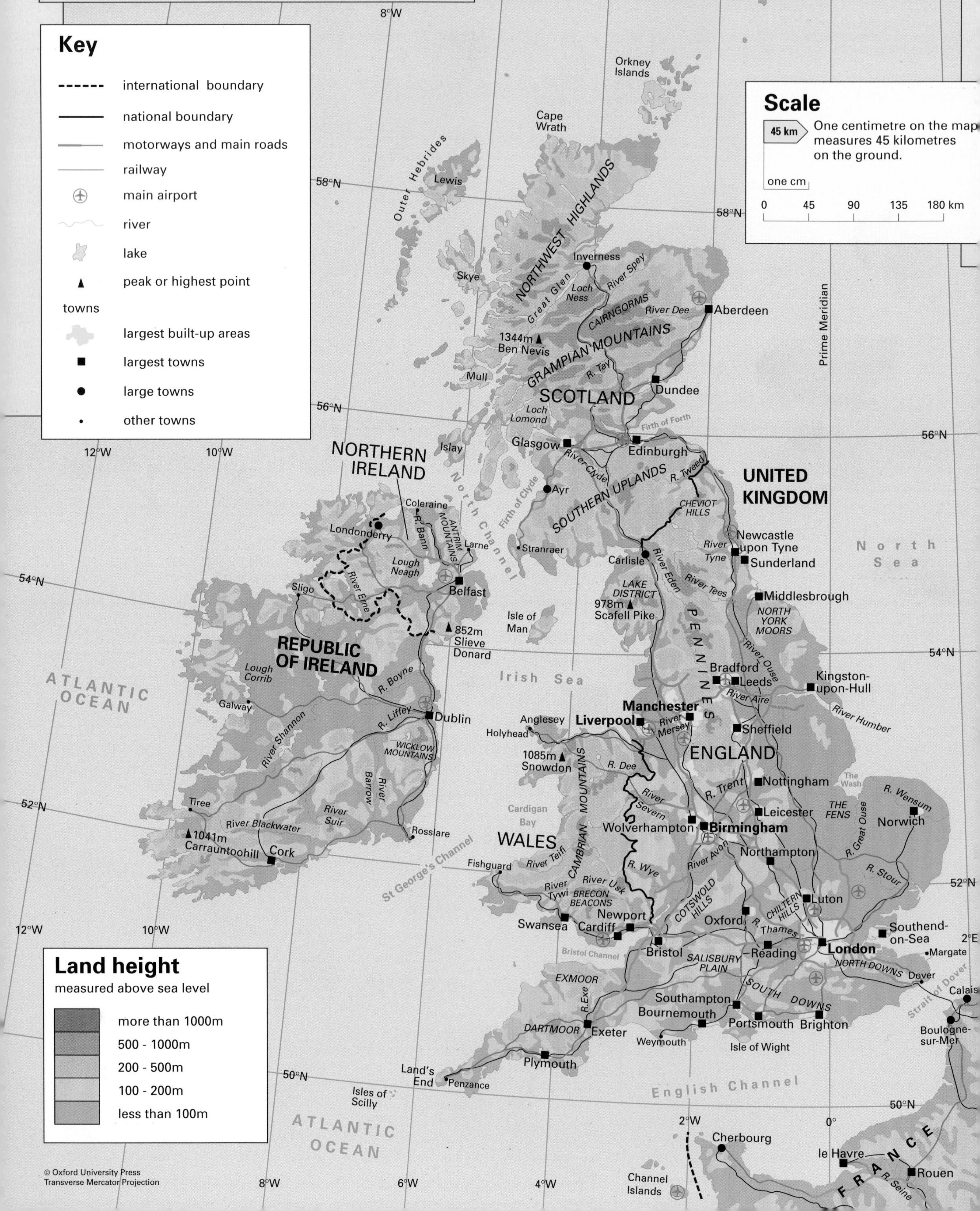

Transverse Mercator Projection

Scale
10 km
One centimetre on the map measures 10 kilometres on the ground.
one cm
0 10 20 30 40 km
Key
county or region boundary
motorway and main roads
railway
main airport
river
lake
peak or highest point
towns
other towns
Land height
measured above sea level
200-500m
100-200m
less than 100m
3°W
2°W
1°W
4°W
60°N
59°N
A
B
C
D
E
1
2
3
ATLANTIC OCEAN
North Sea
Herma Ness
Haroldswick
Unst
Point of Fethaland
Yell Sound
Yell
Fetlar
449m
Esha Ness
St Magnus Bay
Fora Ness
Out Skerries
Muckle Roe
Papa Stour
Whalsay
Symbister
Mainland
SHETLAND ISLANDS
Walls
417m
Foula
The Deeps
Lerwick
Scalloway
Bressay
Sumburgh Head
Fair Isle
Mull Head
Papa Westray
North Ronaldsay
Westray
Sanday
Westray Firth
Rousay
Eday
Brough Head
Stronsay
Stronsay Firth
Shapinsay
Stromness
Mainland
Kirkwall
Scapa
ORKNEY ISLANDS
Ward Hill 479m
Rora Head
Scapa Flow
Hoy
South Ronaldsay
Pentland Firth
Dunnet Head
Stroma
Strathy Point
Duncansby Head
John o' Groats
Thurso
Halkirk
Kirkwall
Transverse Mercator Projection
© Oxford University Press

Scottish Highlands and Islands

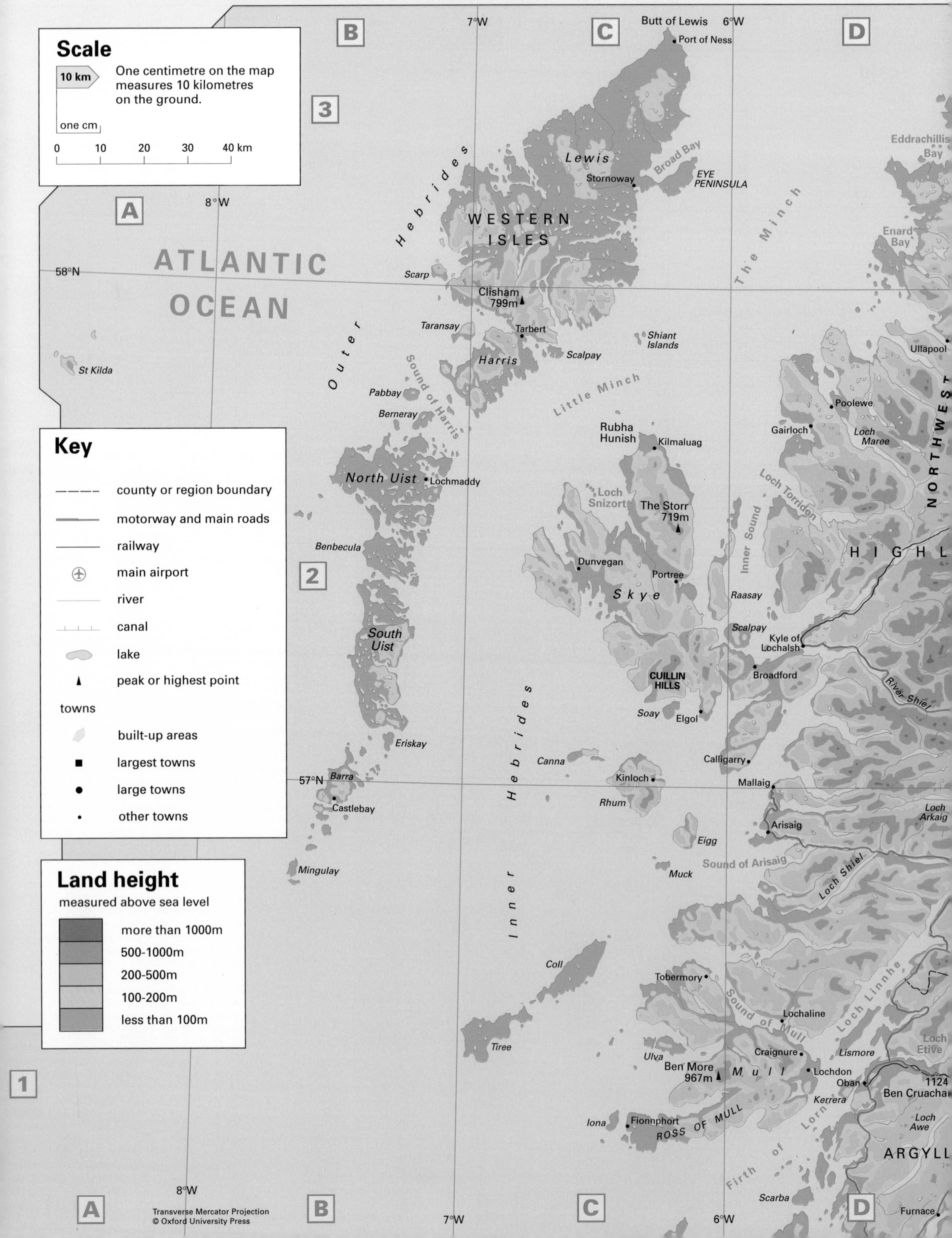
Scale
10 km
One centimetre on the map measures 10 kilometres on the ground.
one cm
0
10
20
30
40 km
Key
county or region boundary
motorway and main roads
railway
main airport
river
canal
lake
peak or highest point
towns
built-up areas
largest towns
large towns
other towns
Land height
measured above sea level
more than 1000m
500-1000m
200-500m
100-200m
less than 100m
A
B
C
D
1
2
3
7°W
6°W
8°W
58°N
57°N
Butt of Lewis
Port of Ness
Lewis
Broad Bay
Stornoway
EYE PENINSULA
WESTERN ISLES
Outer Hebrides
ATLANTIC OCEAN
The Minch
Eddrachillis Bay
Enard Bay
Scarp
Clisham 799m
Taransay
Tarbert
Harris
Scalpay
Shiant Islands
St Kilda
Pabbay
Sound of Harris
Berneray
Little Minch
Ullapool
Poolewe
Gairloch
Loch Maree
NORTHWEST
Rubha Hunish
Kilmaluag
North Uist
Lochmaddy
Loch Snizort
The Storr 719m
Loch Torridon
Inner Sound
Dunvegan
Benbecula
Portree
Skye
Raasay
HIGHL
Scalpay
Kyle of Lochalsh
South Uist
Broadford
CUILLIN HILLS
River Shiel
Soay
Elgol
Inner Hebrides
Eriskay
Canna
Calligarry
Barra
Kinloch
Mallaig
Castlebay
Rhum
Loch Arkaig
Arisaig
Eigg
Sound of Arisaig
Mingulay
Muck
Loch Shiel
Coll
Tobermory
Loch Linnhe
Sound of Mull
Lochaline
Loch Etive
Tiree
Craignure
Lismore
Ulva
Ben More 967m
Mull
Lochdon
Oban
1124
Ben Cruacha
Kerrera
Iona
Fionnphort
ROSS OF MULL
Firth of Lorn
Loch Awe
ARGYLL
Scarba
Furnace

North Sea
Cape Wrath
Strathy Point
Dunnet Head
Stroma
John o' Groats
Thurso
Halkirk
Wick
Loch Eriboll
Ben Hope 927m
HIGHLANDS
River Thurso
Loch nan Clar
Kinbrace
Morven 705m
Lybster
961m Ben Klibreck
River Helmsdale
Helmsdale
998m Ben More Assynt
847m Canisp
Loch Shin
Lairg
Brora
Bonar Bridge
Dornoch
Dornoch Firth
Tarbat Ness
Beinn Dearg 1081m
Tain
1109m Sgurr Mór
1046m Ben Wyvis
Invergordon
Cromarty Firth
Cromarty
Moray Firth
Dingwall
River Meig
Inverness
R. Beauly
Nairn
Forres
Burghead
Branderburgh
Lossiemouth
Elgin
Portknockie
Buckie
Cullen
Portsoy
Banff
Macduff
Rosehearty
Fraserburgh
R. Spey
Fochabers
Aberchirder
Turriff
River Deveron
Keith
Rothes
Charlestown of Aberlour
Dufftown
Huntly
Peterhead
Buchan Ness
Ellon
Oldmeldrum
Inverurie
River Don
Dyce
ABERDEEN CITY
Aberdeen
ABERDEENSHIRE
MORAY
River Nairn
River Spey
Grantown-on-Spey
Loch Mullardoch
Drumnadrochit
Carn Eige 1183m
Loch Ness
Invermoriston
Aviemore
MONADHLIATH MOUNTAINS
Fort Augustus
CAIRNGORMS
1244m Cairn Gorm
Kingussie
Newtonmore
Invergarry
Aboyne
River Dee
Banchory
Ballater
Braemar
Stonehaven
GRAMPIAN MOUNTAINS
1155m Lochnagar
River North Esk
Loch Lochy
Laurencekirk
Inverbervie
Ben Alder 1148m
Fort William 1344m Ben Nevis
Loch Ericht
PERTH AND KINROSS
River Isla
ANGUS
Milton Ness
Blackwater Reservoir
Pitlochry
Brechin
Montrose
River South Esk
Kirriemuir
Loch Rannoch
Forfar
Alyth
River Tay
Aberfeldy
Blairgowrie
Rattray
Arbroath
Ben Lawers 1214m
Loch Tay
Coupar Angus
SIDLAW HILLS
DUNDEE CITY
Dundee
Carnoustie
Tyndrum
Perth
Firth of Tay
Dalmally
Crianlarich
Ben More 1174m
Loch Earn
Crieff
River Earn
Newburgh
St Andrews
SCOTLAND
Cupar
Auchterarder
OCHIL HILLS
Auchtermuchty
ARGYLL AND BUTE
Loch Katrine
M90
FIFE
Crail
Callander
Anstruther
Inveraray
Tarbet
Kinross
Glenrothes
Ben Lomond 974m
STIRLING
Dunblane
CLACKMANNANSHIRE
Loch Leven
Buckhaven
Loch Lomond
River Forth
Stirling
Alloa
Kirkcaldy
Ben Nevis
Aberdeen
5°W
4°W
3°W
2°W
58°
57°
E
F
G
H
1
2
3
Transverse Mercator Projection
© Oxford University Press

Key
international boundary
national boundary
county or region boundary
motorway and main roads
railway
main airport
river
canal
lake
peak or highest point
towns
built-up areas
largest towns
large towns
other towns
Land height
measured above sea level
more than 1000m
500-1000m
200-500m
100-200m
less than 100m
Edinburgh
Belfast
A
B
C
D
2
3
4
8°W
7°W
6°W
5°W
54°N
55°N
56°N
Iona
Fionnphort
ROSS OF MULL
Kerrera
Oban
Dalmally
Loch Awe
Firth of Lorn
Scarba
Inveraray
ARGYLL AND BUT
Furnace
Loch Fyne
Colonsay
Scalasaig
Oronsay
Lochgilphead
Jura
Sound of Jura
Kilmory
Dunoon
Tighnabruaich
Bute
Rothesay
Tarbert
Port Askaig
Craighouse
Islay
Portnahaven
Mull of Oa
Port Ellen
Ardbeg
Gigha
Ardminish
Clachan
Claonaig
Sound of Bute
Lochranza
Goat Fell
874 m
Arran
Brodick
Kilbrannan Sound
Firth of Clyde
KINTYRE
NORTH AYRSHIRE
Campbeltown
Southend
Mull of Kintyre
Rathlin Island
Rathlin Sound
Fair Head
Ailsa Craig
Girva
North Channel
Ballantrae
Corsewall Point
Water of L
Stranraer
Portpatrick
Lu Ba
Drummore
Mull of Galloway
Malin Head
Tory Island
Tory Sound
INISHOWEN PENINSULA
Slieve Snaght
615m
Lough Swilly
Buncrana
Lough Foyle
Errigal Mountain
752m
Creeslough
Kilmacrenan
Letterkenny
R. Swilly
Londonderry
LONDONDERRY
River Foyle
Portrush
Portstewart
Coleraine
COLERAINE
Limavady
LIMAVADY
Dungiven
Ballycastle
MOYLE
River Bush
Ballymoney
BALLYMONEY
ANTRIM MOUNTAINS
River Bann
River Main
BALLYMENA
Ballymena
LARNE
Larne
Island Magee
DONEGAL
River Finn
Ballybofey
Strabane
STRABANE
Sawel
683m
Maghera
MAGHERAFELT
Magherafelt
529m
Lough Beg
ANTRIM
Randalstown
M2
CARRICKFERGUS
Carrickfergus
NEWTOWNABBEY
Antrim
Newtownabbey
Belfast Lough
Bangor
NORTH DOWN
Donaghadee
Donegal
River Derg
Newtownstewart
NORTHERN IRELAND
Cookstown
COOKSTOWN
Lough Neagh
Crumlin
BELFAST
Belfast
Newtownards
CASTLEREAGH
Omagh
OMAGH
Lough Derg
Ballyshannon
Lough Melvin
Lower Lough Erne
Coalisland
Dungannon
DUNGANNON
CRAIGAVON
M1
R. Blackwater
Lisburn
LISBURN
ARDS
Strangford Lough
ARDS PENINSULA
FERMANAGH
Lough Macnean Upper
Lough Macnean Lower
Enniskillen
Lurgan
Craigavon
Portadown
Dromore
Armagh
ARMAGH
Banbridge
River Bann
BANBRIDGE
DOWN
Downpatrick
LEITRIM
R. Shannon
Monaghan
Keady
Slieve Donard
852m
Newcastle
St John's Point
Lough Allen
Upper Lough Erne
Newtownhamilton
Clones
MONAGHAN
Newry
NEWRY AND MOURNE
R. Erne
Castleblayney
Warrenpoint
Crossmaglen
Carlingford Lough
Kilkeel
REPUBLIC OF IRELAND
Lough Oughter
Carrick-on-Shannon
Cavan
CAVAN
LOUTH
Carrickmacross
Dundalk
Transverse Mercator Projection
© Oxford University Press

Scale
10 km
One centimetre on the map measures 10 kilometres on the ground.
one cm
0 10 20 30 40 km
E
F
G
H
4
3
2
1
4°W
3°W
2°W
56°N
55°N
54°N
Crianlarich
1174m Ben More
Loch Earn
Crieff
River Earn
Perth
Newburgh
Cupar
St Andrews
Loch Katrine
Auchterarder
OCHIL HILLS
Auchtermuchty
FIFE
Crail
Anstruther
Callander
Kinross
Glenrothes
Ben Lomond 974m
STIRLING
Dunblane
CLACKMANNAN-SHIRE
Loch Leven
M90
Buckhaven
Loch Long
Loch Lomond
River Forth
Alloa
Stirling
Dunfermline
Kirkcaldy
Firth of Forth
North Berwick
WEST DUNBARTONSHIRE
Grangemouth
Bo'ness
Inverkeithing
Dunbar
Helensburgh
CAMPSIE FELLS
FALKIRK
M9
Falkirk
Edinburgh
EAST LOTHIAN
LAMMERMUIR HILLS
St Abb's Head
North Sea
Greenock
Alexandria
EAST DUNBARTONSHIRE
Dumbarton
Cumbernauld
Linlithgow
CITY OF EDINBURGH
Musselburgh
Eyemouth
Port Glasgow
Clydebank
Bearsden
Kirkintilloch
Bathgate
Livingston
INVERCLYDE
Paisley
Coatbridge
Airdrie
M8
WEST LOTHIAN
MIDLOTHIAN
Glasgow
GLASGOW CITY
NORTH LANARKSHIRE
Penicuik
PENTLAND HILLS
Johnstone
RENFREWSHIRE
Hamilton
Motherwell
Wishaw
Duns
Whiteadder Water
Berwick-upon-Tweed
EAST RENFREWSHIRE
East Kilbride
R. Clyde
M74
Leader Water
River Tweed
Holy Island
Lanark
Peebles
Coldstream
Saltcoats
Kilmarnock
SOUTH LANARKSHIRE
Biggar
Innerleithen
Galashiels
Melrose
Bamburgh
Irvine
Darvel
Kelso
SCOTLAND
SOUTHERN UPLANDS
Selkirk
Troon
EAST AYRSHIRE
River Ayr
River Tweed
Broad Law 840m
Yarrow Water
SCOTTISH BORDERS
Wooler
Prestwick
St Mary's Loch
Jedburgh
815m The Cheviot
Ayr
Cumnock
River Teviot
Hawick
River Aln
Alnwick
New Cumnock
LOWTHER HILLS
Daer Reservoir
Amble
Maybole
River Doon
Sanquhar
Moffat
River Coquet
SOUTH AYRSHIRE
River Nith
602m Peel Fell
CHEVIOT HILLS
River Rede
Thornhill
R. Annan
NORTHUMBERLAND
Ashington
River Stinchar
Loch Doon
River Esk
Kielder Water
River Wansbeck
Blyth
DUMFRIES AND GALLOWAY
Langholm
Liddel Water
River Blyth
Lockerbie
Cramlington
Whitley Bay
St John's Town of Dalry
Lochmaben
Dumfries
River Annan
New Galloway
Loch Ken
Newcastle upon Tyne
South Shields
R. Cree
River Tyne
Annan
Haltwhistle
Hexham
Newton Stewart
Castle Douglas
Dalbeattie
Kirkbean
River Irthing
Brampton
Gateshead
Washington
Sunderland
River Dee
Gatehouse of Fleet
Solway Firth
Carlisle
Consett
Glenluce
Wigtown
River Derwent
Chester-le-Street
Kirkcudbright
Wigton
PENNINES
Durham
Wigtown Bay
River Eden
Cross Fell 893m
River Wear
Spennymoor
Whithorn
M6
Maryport
River Ellen
DURHAM
Bishop Auckland
R.Derwent
Cockermouth
Skiddaw 931m
Penrith
River Tees
Newton Aycliffe
Workington
790m Mickle Fell
DARLINGTON
Keswick
Irish Sea
Derwent Water
CUMBRIA
Whitehaven
Ullswater
Appleby-in-Westmorland
Barnard Castle
Darlington
Brough
Helvellyn 950m
ENGLAND
St Bees Head
LAKE DISTRICT
Kirkby Stephen
River Swale
Scafell Pike 978m
Ambleside
Richmond
Point of Ayre
Windermere
Seascale
Coniston Water
Kendal
River Ure
Leyburn
Snaefell 620m
Ramsey
Kirk Michael
Whernside 737m
NORTH YORKSHIRE
River Lune
R. Greta
Ingleborough 723m
River Wharfe
Peel
ISLE OF MAN
South Barrule 483m
693m Pen-y-Ghent
704m Great Whernside
Ripon
Douglas
Dalton-in-Furness
Morecambe Bay
Carnforth
R. Nidd
Barrow-in-Furness
River Aire
Morecambe
Lancaster
Heysham
560m Ward's Stone
Castletown
Skipton
FOREST OF BOWLAND
Barnoldswick
Ilkley
Transverse Mercator Projection
© Oxford University Press

A
B
C
D
1
2
3
4
55°N
54°N
53°N
4°W
3°W
2°W
Lochmaben
Lockerbie
Langholm
R. Wansbeck
Blyth
Cramlington
NORTHUMBERLAND
Newcastle upon Tyne
Newton Stewart
Castle Douglas
Kirkbean
Dalbeattie
Gatehouse of Fleet
R. Dee
Glenluce
Wigtown
Kirkcudbright
Luce Bay
Wigtown Bay
Whithorn
Drummore
Mull of Galloway
Solway Firth
Annan
M6
River Irthing
Haltwhistle
Hexham
R. Tyne
Brampton
Gateshead
Washington
Carlisle
R. Derwent
Consett
Chester-le-Street
Durham
Wigton
River Eden
Cross Fell 893m
River Wear
Maryport
River Ellen
PENNINES
DURHAM
Spennymoor
Bishop Auckland
Newton Aycliffe
R. Derwent
Cockermouth
931m Skiddaw
Penrith
Workington
Keswick
Derwent Water
CUMBRIA
Mickle Fell 790m
River Tees
Whitehaven
Appleby-in-Westmorland
Barnard Castle
DARLINGTON
Darlington
Helvellyn 950m
Ullswater
St Bees Head
LAKE DISTRICT
Brough
Kirkby Stephen
978m Scafell Pike
Ambleside
Point of Ayre
Seascale
Windermere
Richmond
River Swale
Ramsey
Coniston Water
Kirk Michael
Snaefell 620m
Kendal
R. Ure
Leyburn
Peel
ISLE OF MAN
Whernside 737m
River Lune
NORTH YORKSHIRE
South Barrule 483m
Douglas
River Wharfe
R. Greta
Pen-y-Ghent 693m
Great Whernside 704m
723m Ingleborough
Dalton-in-Furness
Morecambe Bay
Castletown
Barrow-in-Furness
Carnforth
Ripon
River Nidd
Morecambe
Lancaster
Heysham
560m Ward's Stone
FOREST OF BOWLAND
River Aire
Skipton
Harrogate
Fleetwood
Barnoldswick
Ilkley
Keighley
BLACKPOOL
River Wyre
Irish Sea
LANCASHIRE
River Ribble
Nelson
Blackpool
M55
Preston
Burnley
Bradford
Leeds
Lytham St Anne's
Blackburn
Halifax
BLACKBURN WITH DARWEN
WEST
Leyland
Brighouse
Dewsbury
Chorley
Huddersfield
Southport
M62
YORKSHIRE
Bury
Rochdale
Bolton
M61
Formby
Oldham
Skelmersdale
Wigan
GREATER MANCHESTER
Manchester
Kirkby
Carmel Head
Amlwch
Bootle
MERSEYSIDE
Salford
St Helens
Wallasey
Birkenhead
Liverpool
Warrington
Sale
Stockport
The Peak 636m
Holyhead
Widnes
WARRINGTON
Cheadle
M53
ISLE OF ANGLESEY
Llandudno
Rhyl
River Dee
Holy Island
Conwy
Runcorn
HALTON
R. Mersey
Colwyn Bay
Ellesmere Port
Macclesfield
Bangor
R. Conwy
FLINTSHIRE
River Clwyd
Buxton
R. Derwent
Anglesey
Flint
Northwich
Bethesda
Denbigh
CHESHIRE
Bakewell
Chester
DERBYSHIRE
Caernarfon
Mold
River Dove
CONWY
Winsford
Caernarfon Bay
Snowdon 1085m
Matlock
Crewe
DENBIGHSHIRE
Kidsgrove
Wrexham
STOKE-ON-TRENT
Newcastle-under-Lyme
Stoke-on-Trent
Ashbourne
LLEYN PENINSULA
Blaenau Ffestiniog
River Dee
CAMBRIAN MOUNTAINS
WREXHAM
Llangollen
Whitchurch
Portmadog
ENGLAND
Pwllheli
Bala
DERBY CITY
Bala Lake
Harlech
Oswestry
Market Drayton
Uttoxeter
GWYNEDD
Burton upon Trent
Stafford
Lake Vyrnwy
Barmouth
Newport
Rugeley
Dolgellau
R. Vyrnwy
POWYS
TELFORD AND WREKIN
Cader Idris 892m
STAFFORDSHIRE
Cardigan Bay
Telford
Cannock
Welshpool
Shrewsbury
Lichfield
407m The Wrekin
M54
WALES
R. Dyfi
M42
Tamworth
R. Severn
SHROPSHIRE
Machynlleth
Montgomery
Wolverhampton
Walsall

Transverse Mercator Projection

Northern England

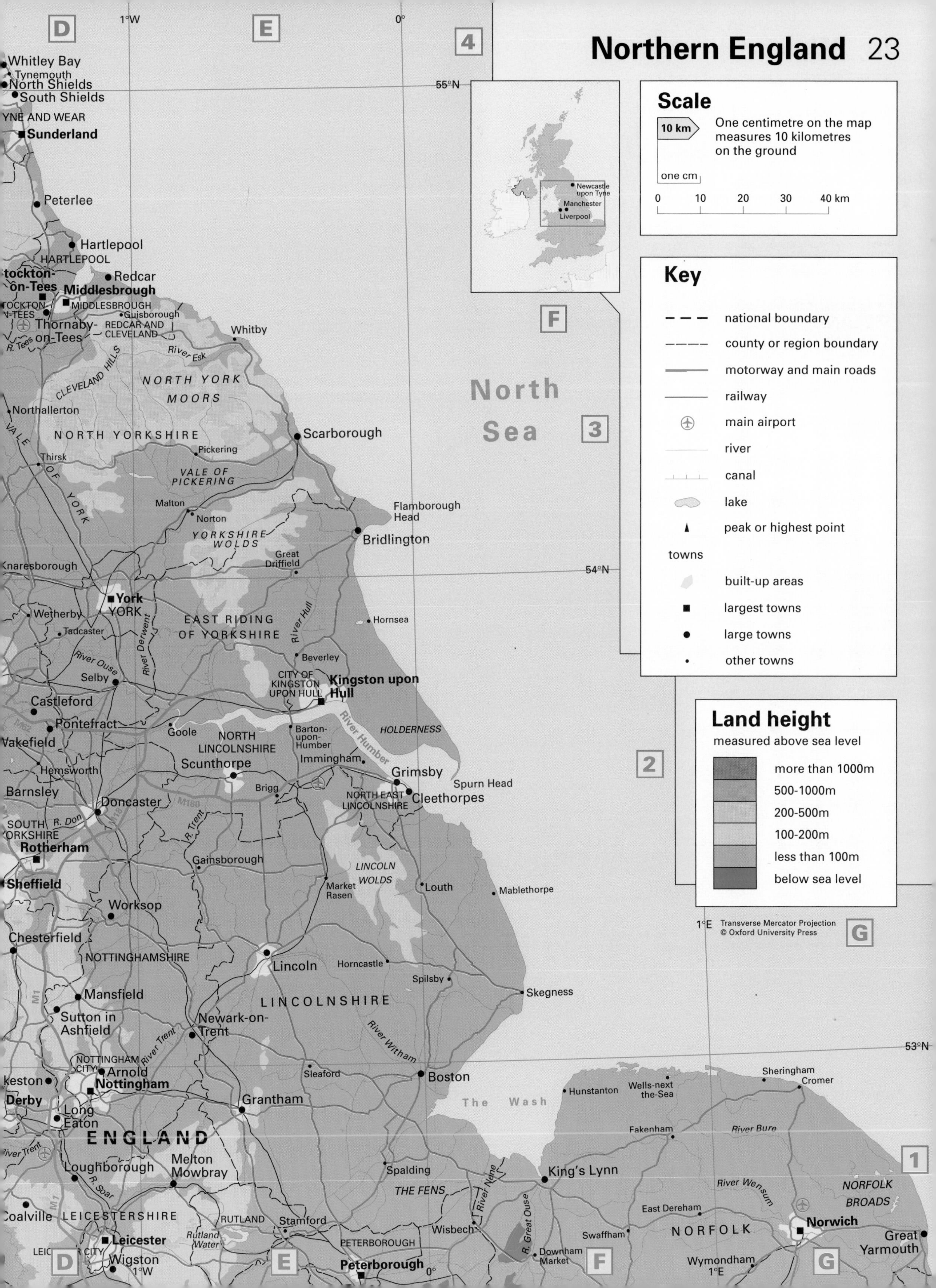

D
E
F
G
1°W
0°
1°E
55°N
54°N
53°N
4
3
2
1
Scale
10 km
one cm
One centimetre on the map measures 10 kilometres on the ground
0 10 20 30 40 km
Newcastle upon Tyne
Manchester
Liverpool
Key
national boundary
county or region boundary
motorway and main roads
railway
main airport
river
canal
lake
peak or highest point
towns
built-up areas
largest towns
large towns
other towns
Land height
measured above sea level
more than 1000m
500-1000m
200-500m
100-200m
less than 100m
below sea level
Transverse Mercator Projection
© Oxford University Press
North Sea
Whitley Bay
Tynemouth
North Shields
South Shields
YNE AND WEAR
Sunderland
Peterlee
Hartlepool
HARTLEPOOL
tockton-on-Tees
Redcar
Middlesbrough
MIDDLESBROUGH
Guisborough
Thornaby-on-Tees
REDCAR AND CLEVELAND
R. Tees
Whitby
River Esk
CLEVELAND HILLS
NORTH YORK MOORS
Northallerton
NORTH YORKSHIRE
VALE OF YORK
Scarborough
Thirsk
Pickering
VALE OF PICKERING
Malton
Norton
Flamborough Head
YORKSHIRE WOLDS
Bridlington
Great Driffield
Knaresborough
York
YORK
Wetherby
Tadcaster
EAST RIDING OF YORKSHIRE
River Hull
River Derwent
Hornsea
River Ouse
Beverley
Selby
CITY OF KINGSTON UPON HULL
Kingston upon Hull
Castleford
Pontefract
M62
Goole
NORTH LINCOLNSHIRE
Barton-upon-Humber
River Humber
HOLDERNESS
Wakefield
Scunthorpe
Immingham
Hemsworth
Grimsby
Spurn Head
Barnsley
Brigg
NORTH EAST LINCOLNSHIRE
Cleethorpes
Doncaster
M180
M18
R. Don
R. Trent
SOUTH YORKSHIRE
Rotherham
Gainsborough
LINCOLN WOLDS
Sheffield
Market Rasen
Louth
Mablethorpe
Worksop
Chesterfield
NOTTINGHAMSHIRE
Lincoln
Horncastle
Spilsby
Mansfield
M1
Skegness
LINCOLNSHIRE
Sutton in Ashfield
Newark-on-Trent
River Trent
River Witham
NOTTINGHAM CITY
Arnold
Nottingham
Sleaford
Boston
Ilkeston
Derby
Grantham
The Wash
Long Eaton
ENGLAND
River Trent
Hunstanton
Wells-next-the-Sea
Sheringham
Cromer
Fakenham
River Bure
Loughborough
Melton Mowbray
Spalding
King's Lynn
R. Soar
THE FENS
River Nene
River Wensum
NORFOLK BROADS
Coalville
LEICESTERSHIRE
RUTLAND
Stamford
Wisbech
R. Great Ouse
East Dereham
Norwich
Leicester
Rutland Water
Swaffham
NORFOLK
Great Yarmouth
LEICESTER CITY
Wigston
PETERBOROUGH
Peterborough
Downham Market
Wymondham

Irish Sea
Irish Sea
ATLANTIC OCEAN
Bristol Channel
St George's Channel
Cardigan Bay
Caernarfon Bay
Carmarthen Bay
St Brides Bay
Bridgwater Bay
REPUBLIC OF IRELAND
Dublin
Dún Laoghaire
Malahide
Howth
Bray
Greystones
Wicklow
Arklow
WALES
ISLE OF ANGLESEY
Anglesey
Holy Island
Holyhead
Carmel Head
Amlwch
Bangor
Bethesda
Caernarfon
Snowdon 1085m
LLEYN PENINSULA
Porthmadog
Pwllheli
Harlech
Blaenau Ffestiniog
Llandudno
Conwy
Colwyn Bay
Rhyl
R. Conwy
CONWY
River Clwyd
Denbigh
DENBIGHSHIRE
FLINTSHIRE
Flint
Mold
Wrexham
WREXHAM
River Dee
Llangollen
Bala
Bala Lake
Oswestry
GWYNEDD
Aran Fawddy 905m
Lake Vyrnwy
R. Vyrnwy
Barmouth
Dolgellau
Cader Idris 892m
Welshpool
R. Dyfi
Machynlleth
CAMBRIAN MOUNTAINS
Montgomery
R. Severn
Newtown
Plynlimon 752m
Llanidloes
SHROPSHIRE
Aberystwyth
CEREDIGION
Rhayader
Knighton
Aberaeron
New Quay
River Teifi
Llandrindod Wells
POWYS
Kington
Builth Wells
R. Wye
Hay-on-Wye
MYNYDD EPPYNT
Lampeter
Cemaes Head
Cardigan
Newcastle Emlyn
Strumble Head
Fishguard
MYNYDD PRESELI
Llandovery
R. Tywi
River Usk
Brecon
811m
BLACK MOUNTAINS
St David's Head
St David's
PEMBROKESHIRE
CARMARTHENSHIRE
Carmarthen
Llandeilo
BRECON BEACONS 886m
Abergavenny
Haverfordwest
Ammanford
Milford Haven
Pembroke
Tenby
Kidwelly
Burry Port
Pontardulais
Llanelli
SWANSEA
Swansea
GOWER
Worms Head
NEATH PORT TALBOT
Neath
Port Talbot
Merthyr Tydfil
MERTHYR TYDFIL
Aberdare
RHONDDA CYNON TAFF
Rhondda
Pontypridd
Caerphilly
CAERPHILLY
Ebbw Vale
BLAENAU GWENT
TORFAEN
Abertillery
Pontypool
Cwmbran
Newport
NEWPORT
BRIDGEND
Bridgend
CARDIFF
Cardiff
THE VALE OF GLAMORGAN
Barry
M4
Weston-super-Mare
Formby
MERSEYSIDE
Bootle
Wallasey
Liverpool
Birkenhead
M53
Ilfracombe
Lynton
Lundy
DEVON
EXMOOR
Dunkery Beacon 519m
Minehead
SOMERSET
6°W
5°W
4°W
3°W
53°N
52°N
A
B
C
D
1
2
3

Transverse Mercator Projection

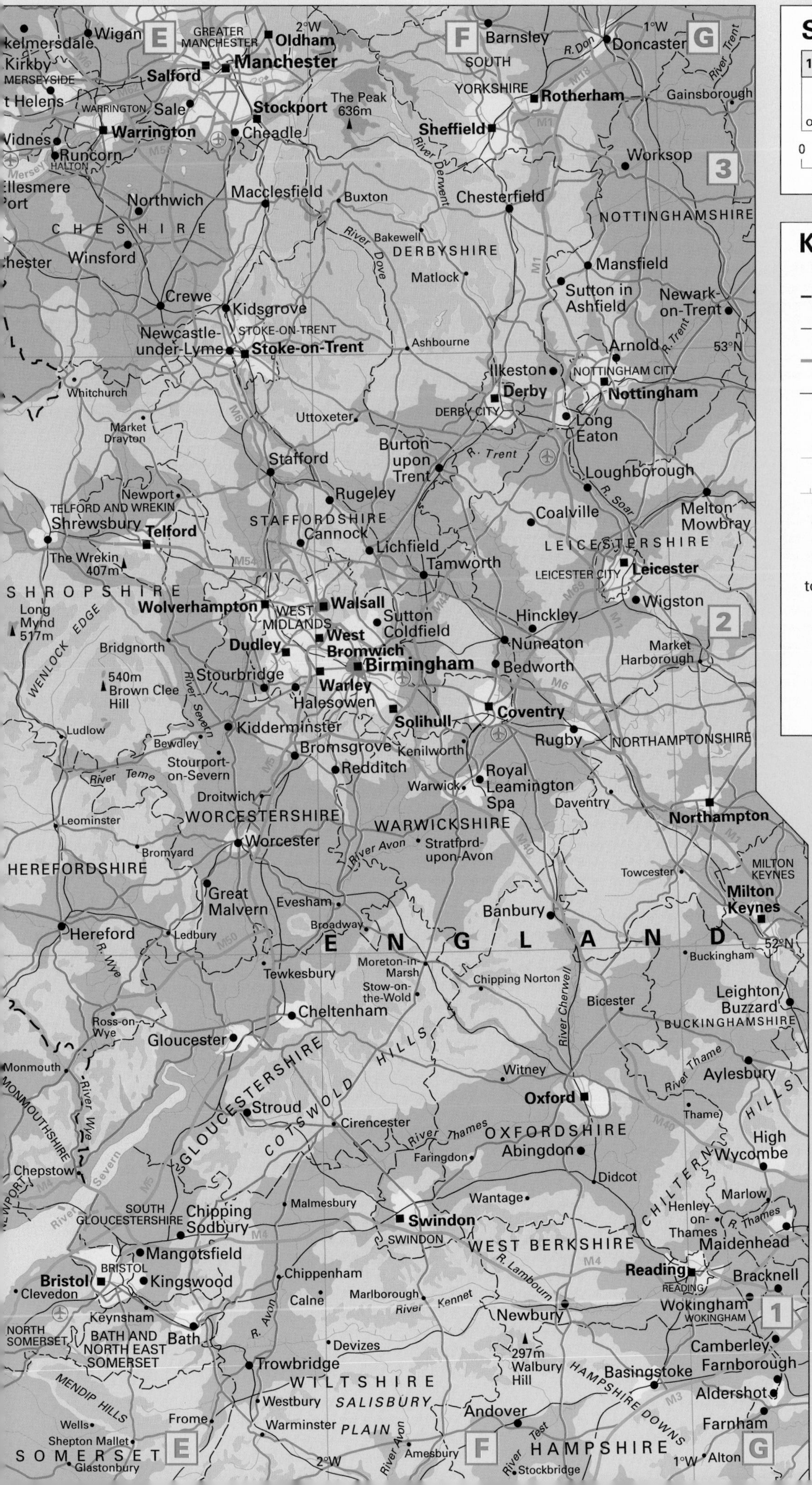

Scale

10 km

one cm

One centimetre on the map measures 10 kilometres on the ground.

0 10 20 30 40 km

Key

- national boundary
- county or region boundary
- motorway and main roads
- railway
- main airport
- river
- canal
- lake
- peak or highest point

towns

- built-up areas
- largest towns
- large towns
- other towns

Land height

measured above sea level

- more than 1000m
- 500-1000m
- 200-500m
- 100-200m
- less than 100m

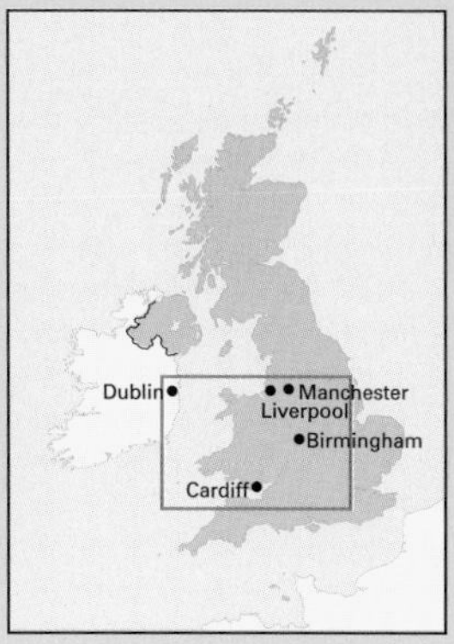

Transverse Mercator Projection

South East England

Scale
10 km
One centimetre on the map measures 10 kilometres on the ground.
one cm
0 10 20 30 40 km
A B C D
1 2 3 4
3°W 2°W 1°W 0°
53°N 52°N 51°N
LINCOLNSHIRE
NOTTINGHAM CITY
Arnold
Nottingham
Ilkeston
River Trent
R. Witham
Sleaford
Boston
DERBY CITY
Derby
Uttoxeter
Long Eaton
Grantham
Burton upon Trent
R. Trent
Melton Mowbray
Spalding
THE FEN
Rugeley
Loughborough
R. Soar
STAFFORDSHIRE
Cannock
Lichfield
Coalville
LEICESTERSHIRE
RUTLAND
Stamford
Tamworth
LEICESTER CITY
Leicester
Rutland Water
PETERBOROUGH
Walsall
WEST MIDLANDS
Sutton Coldfield
Wigston
River Welland
Peterborough
West Bromwich
Hinckley
Dudley
Nuneaton
M1
M69
M42
540m
Brown Clee Hill
Stourbridge
Birmingham
Bedworth
Market Harborough
Corby
Oundle
R. Severn
Warley
Halesowen
M6
Ludlow
Kidderminster
Solihull
Coventry
Kettering
River Nene
Knighton
Bewdley
Bromsgrove
Kenilworth
Rugby
CAMBRIDGESHIRE
Huntingdon
Stourport-on-Severn
River Teme
Redditch
Royal Leamington Spa
M45
Wellingborough
St Ives
Droitwich
Warwick
Leominster
Daventry
NORTHAMPTONSHIRE
Kington
WORCESTERSHIRE
WARWICKSHIRE
Northampton
R. Great Ouse
Bromyard
Worcester
R. Avon
Stratford-upon-Avon
St Neots
HEREFORDSHIRE
M40
Great Malvern
Towcester
MILTON KEYNES
Bedford
Hay-on-Wye
Evesham
Milton Keynes
Biggleswade
Hereford
Broadway
Banbury
BEDFORDSHIRE
Royston
Ledbury
M50
R. Wye
52°N
BLACK MOUNTAINS
811m
ENGLAND
Tewkesbury
Moreton-in-Marsh
Buckingham
Letchworth
Stow-on-the-Wold
Chipping Norton
Hitchin
Ross-on-Wye
Cheltenham
River Cherwell
Bicester
Leighton Buzzard
LUTON
Luton
Stevenage
Abergavenny
Gloucester
BUCKINGHAMSHIRE
Dunstable
HERTFORDSHIRE
Monmouth
COTSWOLD HILLS
Welwyn Garden City
MONMOUTHSHIRE
GLOUCESTERSHIRE
Witney
River Thame
Aylesbury
Abertillery
Stroud
Oxford
A1(M)
TORFAEN
Pontypool
Cirencester
River Thames
Thame
Hemel Hempstead
St Albans
Cwmbran
OXFORDSHIRE
CHILTERN HILLS
Cheshunt
Chepstow
Faringdon
Watford
M25
Enfield
M4
River Severn
Abingdon
High Wycombe
Barnet
Newport
NEWPORT
M5
Didcot
Waltham Forest
SOUTH GLOUCESTERSHIRE
Chipping Sodbury
Malmesbury
Wantage
Harrow
Brent
Marlow
M40
GREATER
Swindon
SWINDON
Henley-on-Thames
R. Thames
Maidenhead
Hillingdon
London
Mangotsfield
WINDSOR AND MAIDENHEAD
SLOUGH
Slough
Ealing
BRISTOL
WEST BERKSHIRE
Clevedon
Bristol
Kingswood
Chippenham
R. Lambourn
Windsor
Greenwich
Calne
Reading
READING
Bracknell
Hounslow
Richmond upon Thames
Weston-super-Mare
Keynsham
Marlborough
River Kennet
Wokingham
Staines
LONDON
NORTH SOMERSET
BATH AND NORTH EAST SOMERSET
Bath
Newbury
WOKINGHAM
BRACKNELL FOREST
Kingston upon Thames
Merton
Sutton
Devizes
297m
Walbury Hill
M3
Camberley
Croydon
MENDIP HILLS
Trowbridge
Epsom
WILTSHIRE
Basingstoke
Woking
SURREY
Westbury
SALISBURY PLAIN
HAMPSHIRE DOWNS
Aldershot
Farnborough
Reigate
M25
Wells
Frome
Guildford
Redhill
Warminster
Andover
Farnham
Dorking
Shepton Mallet
Amesbury
NORTH DOWNS
M23
Bridgwater
Glastonbury
River Test
Alton
294m
Leith Hill
SOMERSET
R. Parrett
Mere
Stockbridge
R. Itchen
Haslemere
Crawley
Wincanton
Salisbury
Winchester
R. Tone
River Yeo
Horsham
51°N
Shaftesbury
HAMPSHIRE
R. Arun
Ilchester
Romsey
Haywards Heath
Yeovil
Eastleigh
River Meon
Petersfield
WEST SUSSEX
Ilminster
Sherborne
Crewkerne
River Avon
Totton
SOUTH DOWNS
Chard
River Stour
Southampton
SOUTHAMPTON
Waterlooville
M27
Lewes
River Axe
Blandford Forum
Wimborne Minster
Havant
Arundel
BRIGHTON AND HOVE
SOUTH
Axminster
DORSET
Ringwood
Fawley
Fareham
PORTSMOUTH
Chichester
Worthing
Hove
Bridport
POOLE
BOURNEMOUTH
Lymington
Cowes
Gosport
Portsmouth
Littlehampton
Brighton
Lyme Regis
Poole
Christchurch
The Solent
Bognor Regis
Seaton
Dorchester
River Frome
Bournemouth
Ryde
Lyme Bay
Wareham
Newport
Selsey Bill
The Needles
ISLE OF WIGHT
Sandown
Weymouth
Swanage
Shanklin
Portland Bill
St Alban's Head
St Catherine's Point
Transverse Mercator Projection
© Oxford University Press

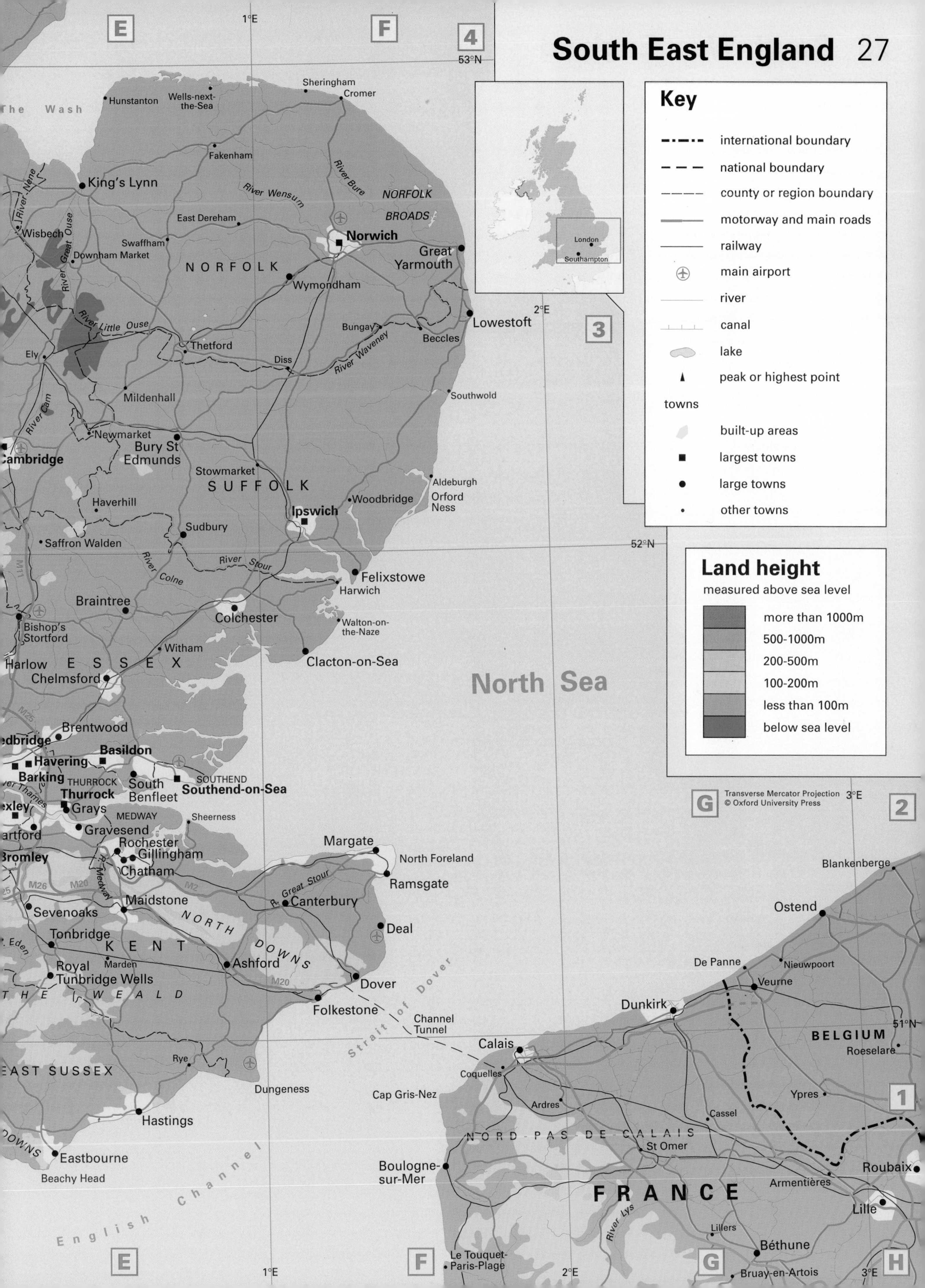
Key
international boundary
national boundary
county or region boundary
motorway and main roads
railway
main airport
river
canal
lake
peak or highest point
towns
built-up areas
largest towns
large towns
other towns
Land height
measured above sea level
more than 1000m
500-1000m
200-500m
100-200m
less than 100m
below sea level
Transverse Mercator Projection
© Oxford University Press
London
Southampton
E
F
G
H
4
3
2
1
1°E
2°E
3°E
53°N
52°N
51°N
The Wash
Hunstanton
Wells-next-the-Sea
Sheringham
Cromer
Fakenham
King's Lynn
River Nene
River Great Ouse
River Wensum
River Bure
NORFOLK BROADS
Wisbech
East Dereham
Norwich
Swaffham
Downham Market
NORFOLK
Great Yarmouth
Wymondham
River Little Ouse
Bungay
Lowestoft
Beccles
Thetford
Ely
Diss
River Waveney
Mildenhall
Southwold
River Cam
Newmarket
Bury St Edmunds
Cambridge
Stowmarket
SUFFOLK
Aldeburgh
Orford Ness
Woodbridge
Haverhill
Ipswich
Sudbury
Saffron Walden
River Colne
River Stour
Felixstowe
Harwich
M11
Braintree
Colchester
Bishop's Stortford
Walton-on-the-Naze
Witham
Clacton-on-Sea
Harlow
ESSEX
Chelmsford
North Sea
M25
Brentwood
Redbridge
Havering
Basildon
Barking
THURROCK
South Benfleet
SOUTHEND
Southend-on-Sea
River Thames
Thurrock
Bexley
Grays
MEDWAY
Sheerness
Dartford
Gravesend
Rochester
Gillingham
Margate
North Foreland
Bromley
R. Medway
Chatham
Ramsgate
M26
M20
M2
Great Stour
Maidstone
Canterbury
Sevenoaks
NORTH DOWNS
Deal
Tonbridge
R. Eden
KENT
Ashford
Royal Tunbridge Wells
Marden
M20
Dover
THE WEALD
Folkestone
Strait of Dover
Channel Tunnel
Calais
Rye
EAST SUSSEX
Coquelles
Dungeness
Cap Gris-Nez
Hastings
DOWNS
Eastbourne
Beachy Head
English Channel
Boulogne-sur-Mer
Le Touquet-Paris-Plage
Blankenberge
Ostend
De Panne
Nieuwpoort
Veurne
Dunkirk
BELGIUM
Roeselare
Ypres
Ardres
Cassel
NORD-PAS-DE-CALAIS
St Omer
Roubaix
Armentières
FRANCE
Lille
River Lys
Lillers
Béthune
Bruay-en-Artois

28 South West England

Scale
10 km
One centimetre on the map measures 10 kilometres on the ground.
one cm
0 10 20 30 40 km
Key
international boundary
national boundary
county or region boundary
motorway and main roads
railway
main airport
river
canal
lake
peak or highest point
towns
built-up areas
largest towns
large towns
other towns
Land height
measured above sea level
more than 1000m
500-1000m
200-500m
100-200m
less than 100m
ATLANTIC
OCEAN
Bristol Channel
THE VALE OF GLAMORG.
Bridger
Lundy
Lynton
Ilfracombe
Minehead
Dunkery Beacon 519m
River Exe
EXMOOR
Braunton
Barnstaple
Bideford Bay
South Molton
Hartland Point
Bideford
River Taw
Great Torrington
River Torridge
Tiverton
DEVON
Cullompton
Bude Bay
Bude
Holsworthy
Hatherleigh
Crediton
M5
Okehampton
Boscastle
Yes Tor 619
River Teign
Exeter
Launceston
Brown Willy 420m
BODMIN MOOR
DARTMOOR
Exmouth
River Tavy
R. Tamar
Dawlish
Bovey Tracey
Teignmouth
Trevose Head
Padstow
River Camel
Wadebridge
Tavistock
Newton Abbot
Buckfastleigh
R. Dart
Bodmin
River Fowey
Liskeard
Torbay
Newquay
CORNWALL
Lostwithiel
Saltash
PLYMOUTH
TORBAY
Totnes
Brixham
Torpoint
Plymouth
Fowey
Looe
St Agnes
St Austell
Fal
Dartmouth
River
Truro
Kingsbridge
St Ives
Redruth
Camborne
Bigbury Bay
Start Bay
Salcombe
Start Point
Penryn
St Just
Penzance
Falmouth
Sennen
Land's End
Mount's Bay
Helston
Mullion
St Martin's
Bryher
Tresco
St Mary's
Hugh Town
Isles of Scilly
Lizard
Lizard Point
ATLANTIC OCEAN
51°N
50°N
49°N
6°W
5°W
4°W
A
B
C
D
1
2
3
4
Transverse Mercator Projection
© Oxford University Press

D
E
F
G
Cardiff
Barry
Clevedon
Mangotsfield
BRISTOL
Bristol
Kingswood
Chippenham
Calne
Keynsham
Bath
NORTH SOMERSET
BATH AND NORTH EAST SOMERSET
Weston-super-Mare
Bridgwater Bay
Devizes
Trowbridge
WILTSHIRE
Westbury
SALISBURY PLAIN
Warminster
Frome
MENDIP HILLS
Wells
Shepton Mallet
Glastonbury
QUANTOCK HILLS
Bridgwater
R. Parrett
SOMERSET
Taunton
Wellington
River Tone
River Yeo
Ilchester
Yeovil
Sherborne
Wincanton
Mere
Shaftesbury
Salisbury
Amesbury
R. Avon
297m Walbury Hill
HAMPSHIRE DOWNS
Basingstoke
Andover
River Test
Stockbridge
R. Itchen
Winchester
HAMPSHIRE
Romsey
Eastleigh
River Meon
Camberley
Farnborough
Aldershot
Farnham
Woking
Guildford
SURREY
Epsom
Dorking
NORTH DOWNS
Alton
Haslemere
R. Arun
Horsham
Petersfield
WEST SUSSEX
SOUTH DOWNS
Arundel
Worthing
Chichester
Littlehampton
Bognor Regis
Selsey Bill
Waterlooville
Havant
Fareham
Gosport
PORTSMOUTH
Portsmouth
Totton
Southampton
SOUTHAMPTON
Fawley
Lymington
The Solent
Cowes
Ryde
Newport
ISLE OF WIGHT
Sandown
Shanklin
St Catherine's Point
The Needles
Christchurch
BOURNEMOUTH
Bournemouth
POOLE
Poole
Ringwood
River Avon
Wimborne Minster
River Stour
Blandford Forum
DORSET
Wareham
River Frome
Swanage
St Alban's Head
Dorchester
Weymouth
Portland Bill
Bridport
Lyme Regis
Lyme Bay
Seaton
Sidmouth
Axminster
River Axe
Chard
Crewkerne
Ilminster
Honiton
M5
M4
M3
M27
English Channel
Alderney
Auderville
Cap de la Hague
Barfleur
Cherbourg
Baie de la Seine
Valognes
FRANCE
Guernsey
St Peter Port
Sark
CHANNEL ISLANDS
Jersey
St Helier
Carteret
Carentan
Isigny-sur-Mer
Lessay
River Vire
St-Lô
Coutainville
Coutances
Caen
River Orne
Cardiff
Southampton
Isles of Scilly
Channel Islands
3°W
2°W
1°W
51°N
50°N
49°N
1
2
3
4
Transverse Mercator Projection
© Oxford University Press

The United Kingdom People and cities

Most people in the United Kingdom live in large towns or cities.

Total number of people, 1991	
England	48 million
Scotland	5 million
Wales	3 million
N. Ireland	2 million
U.K.	**58 million**

More than 250 people live in this square kilometre.

About 100 people live in this square kilometre.

Fewer than 50 people live in this square kilometre.

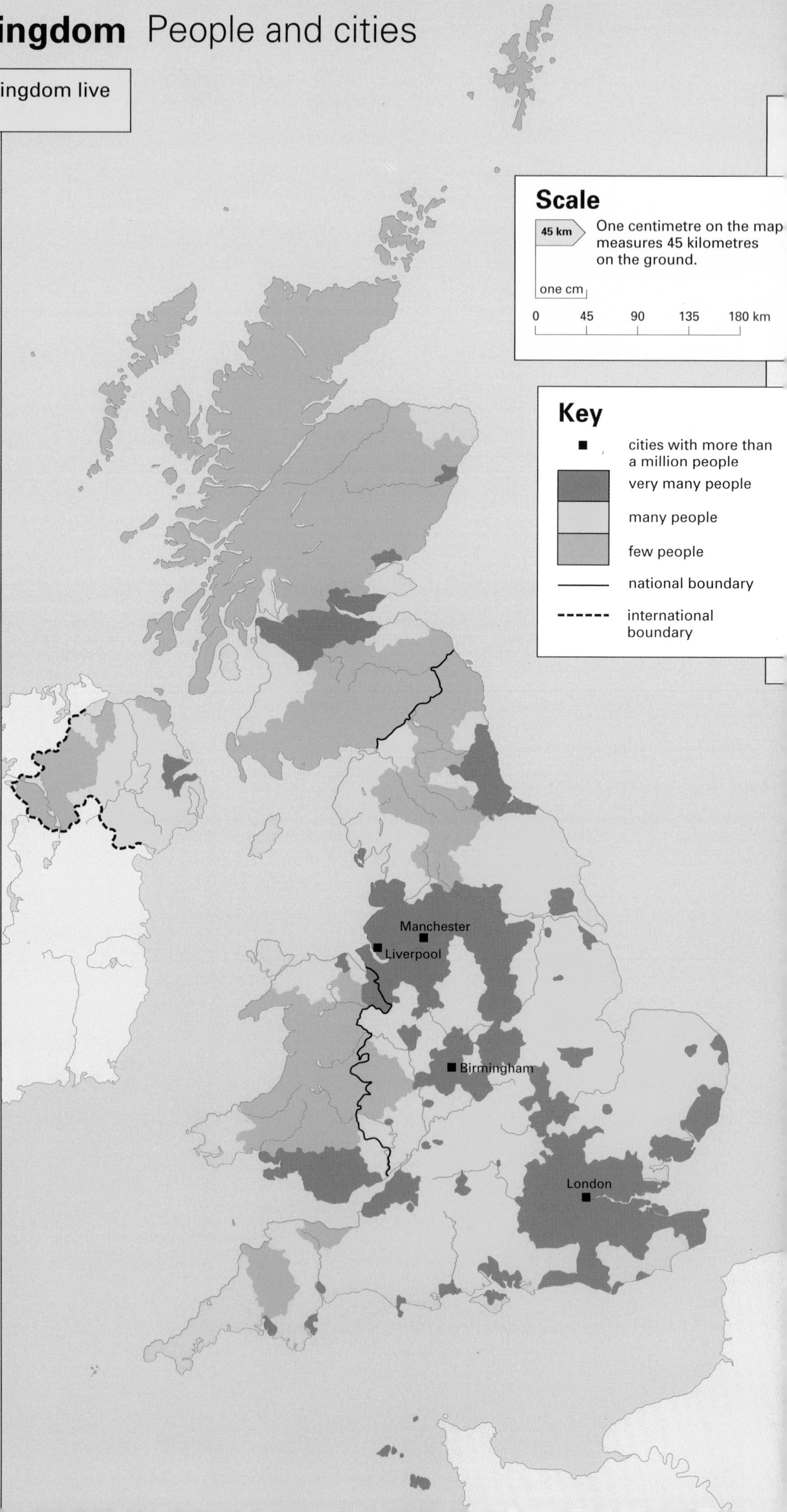

Scale

45 km

One centimetre on the map measures 45 kilometres on the ground.

one cm

0 45 90 135 180 km

Key

- ■ cities with more than a million people
- very many people
- many people
- few people
- national boundary
- international boundary

Transverse Mercator Projection

Farmers produce food by growing crops and keeping animals.

Scale

45 km — One centimetre on the map measures 45 kilometres on the ground.

one cm

0 45 90 135 180 km

Key

	mostly livestock farms	cattle are kept for meat
	mostly hill farms	sheep are kept for meat and wool
	mostly dairy farms	cows are kept for milk
	mostly arable farms	crops are grown

Many farms in Britain are mixed farms. Farmers grow crops *and* keep animals.

(tree symbol)	forestry	trees are planted for wood
(star symbol)	market gardening	fruit and vegetables are grown
	no farming	built-up areas

Transverse Mercator Projection

The United Kingdom Factories and offices

More people work in offices than in factories in the United Kingdom.

Scale

45 km — One centimetre on the map measures 45 kilometres on the ground.

one cm

0 45 90 135 180 km

Key

- major industrial area
- • office and business centre
- —— national boundary
- ------- international boundary

Jobs change

Over time some industries close down.
People lose their jobs.

New industries are often based on high technology but not everyone can find work.

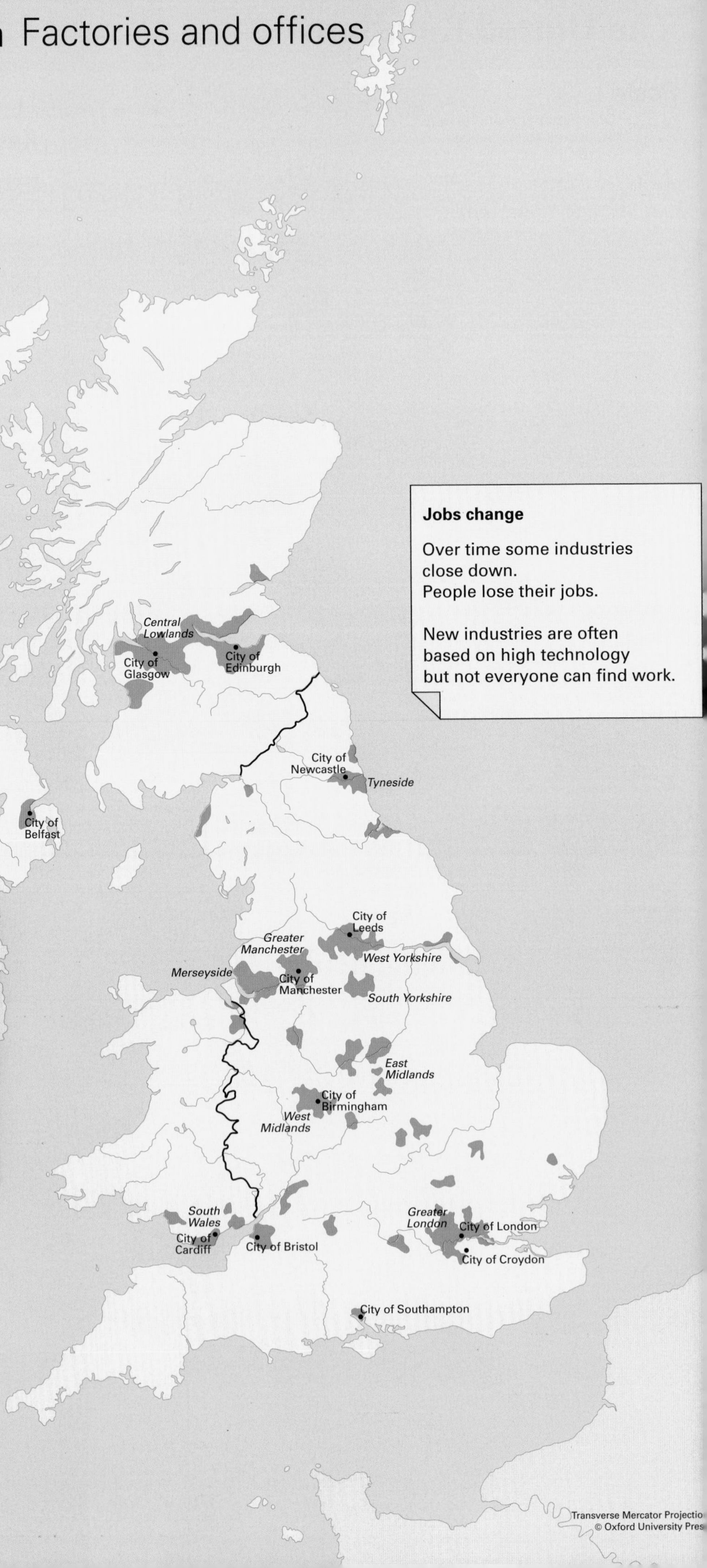

Coal, oil, and natural gas hold energy which originally came from the sun.

Scale

60 km

One centimetre on the map measures 60 kilometres on the ground.

one cm

0 60 120 180 240 km

Oil and gas fields have drilling and pumping rigs

Key

- ● largest coal mines
- gas field and pipeline
- oil field and pipeline

largest power stations

- ▲ burning coal, oil or gas
- ▲ using water power
- ▲ using nuclear power
- △ using wind power

△ wind generator

▲ power station burning coal

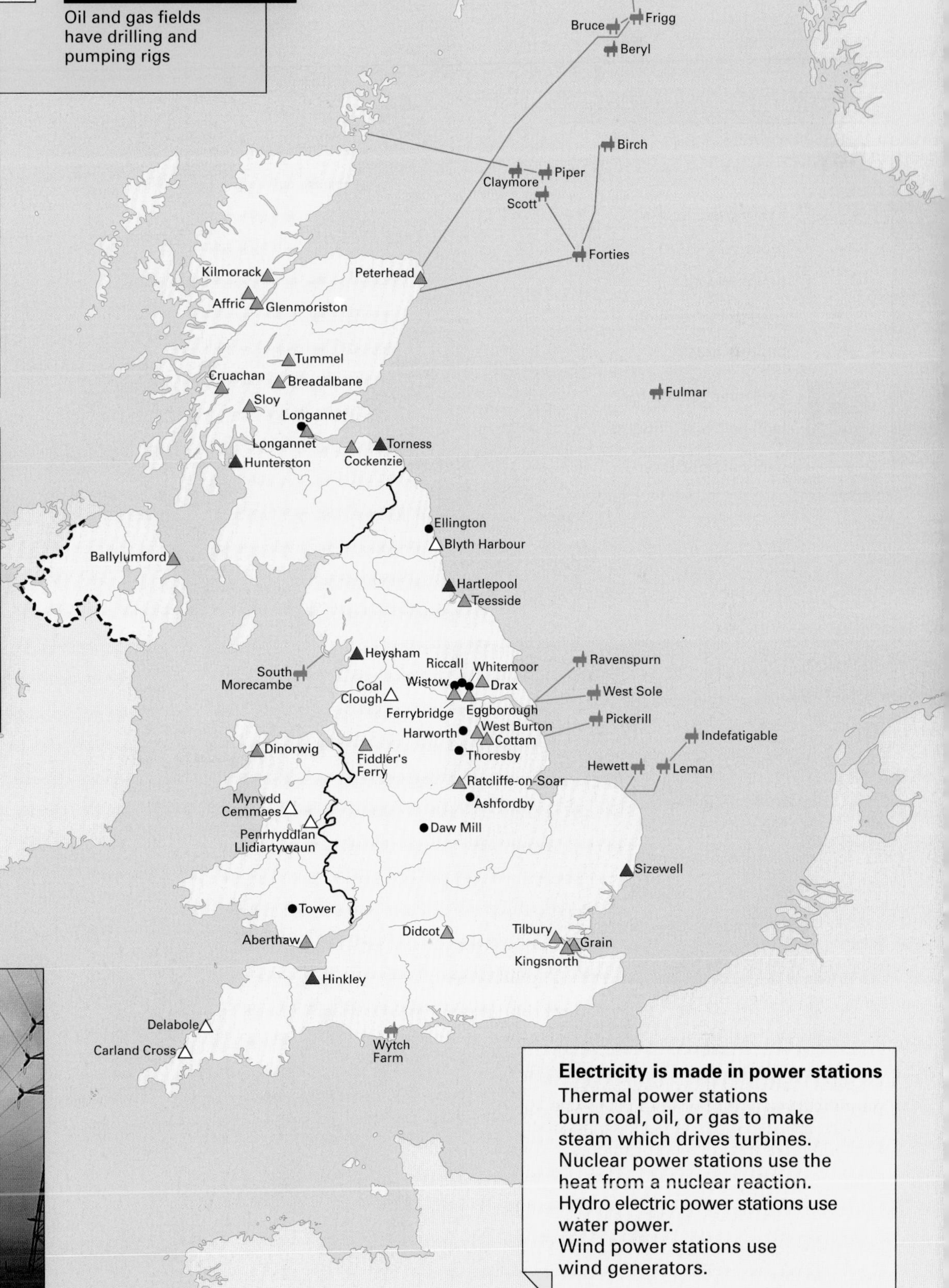

Electricity is made in power stations

Thermal power stations burn coal, oil, or gas to make steam which drives turbines.
Nuclear power stations use the heat from a nuclear reaction.
Hydro electric power stations use water power.
Wind power stations use wind generators.

Transverse Mercator Projection

The United Kingdom Roads and railways

Roads and railways do not always take the shortest route between places.

Scale

45 km — One centimetre on the map measures 45 kilometres on the ground.

one cm

0 45 90 135 180 km

Key

- major road
- motorway
- main railway
- road or rail terminal
- built-up areas
- land over 200 metres
- land below 200 metres
- national boundary

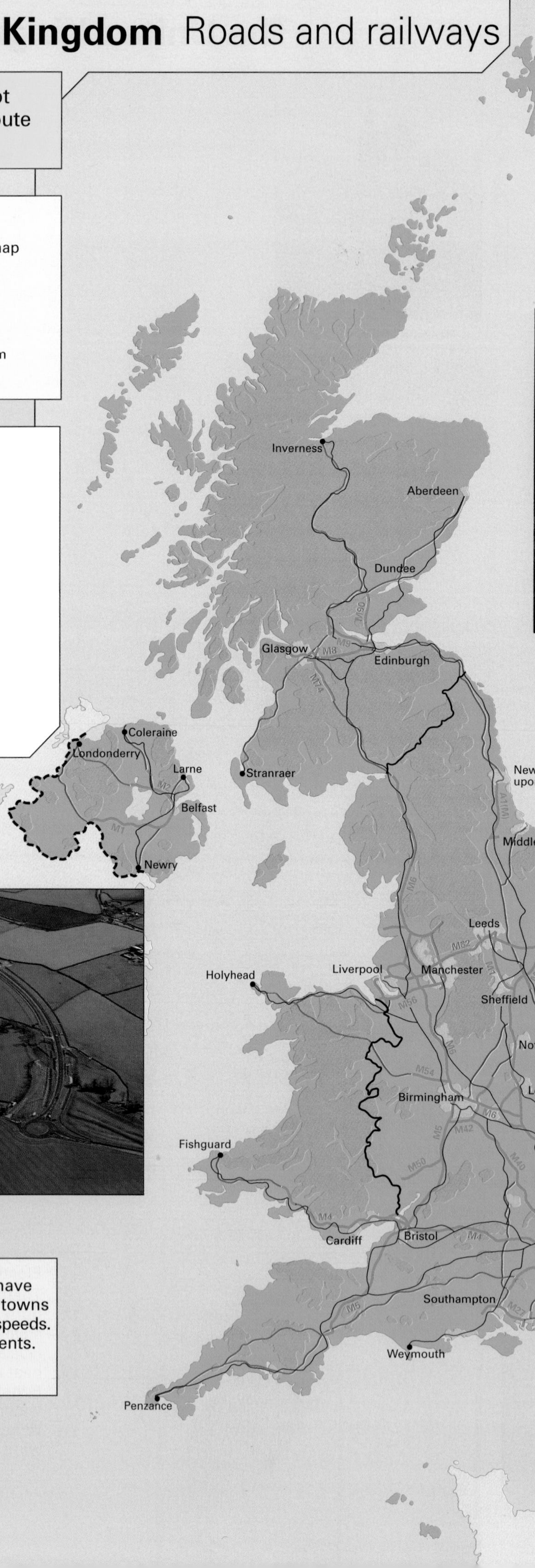

valley of the River Taff near Cardiff, South Wales

bypass, Cannington, Somerset

Modern roads and motorways have gentle curves and often bypass towns to allow traffic to move at higher speeds. Rail networks avoid steep gradients.

Transverse Mercator Projection

Key

- country boundary
- main United Kingdom airways
- other airways
- major United Kingdom airport
- other major airport
- car ferry route
- major car ferry port
- major United Kingdom sea port
- built-up areas

Scale

90 km — One centimetre on the map measures 90 kilometres on the ground.

one cm

0 90 180 270 360 km

Ports and airports link the United Kingdom with the rest of the world.

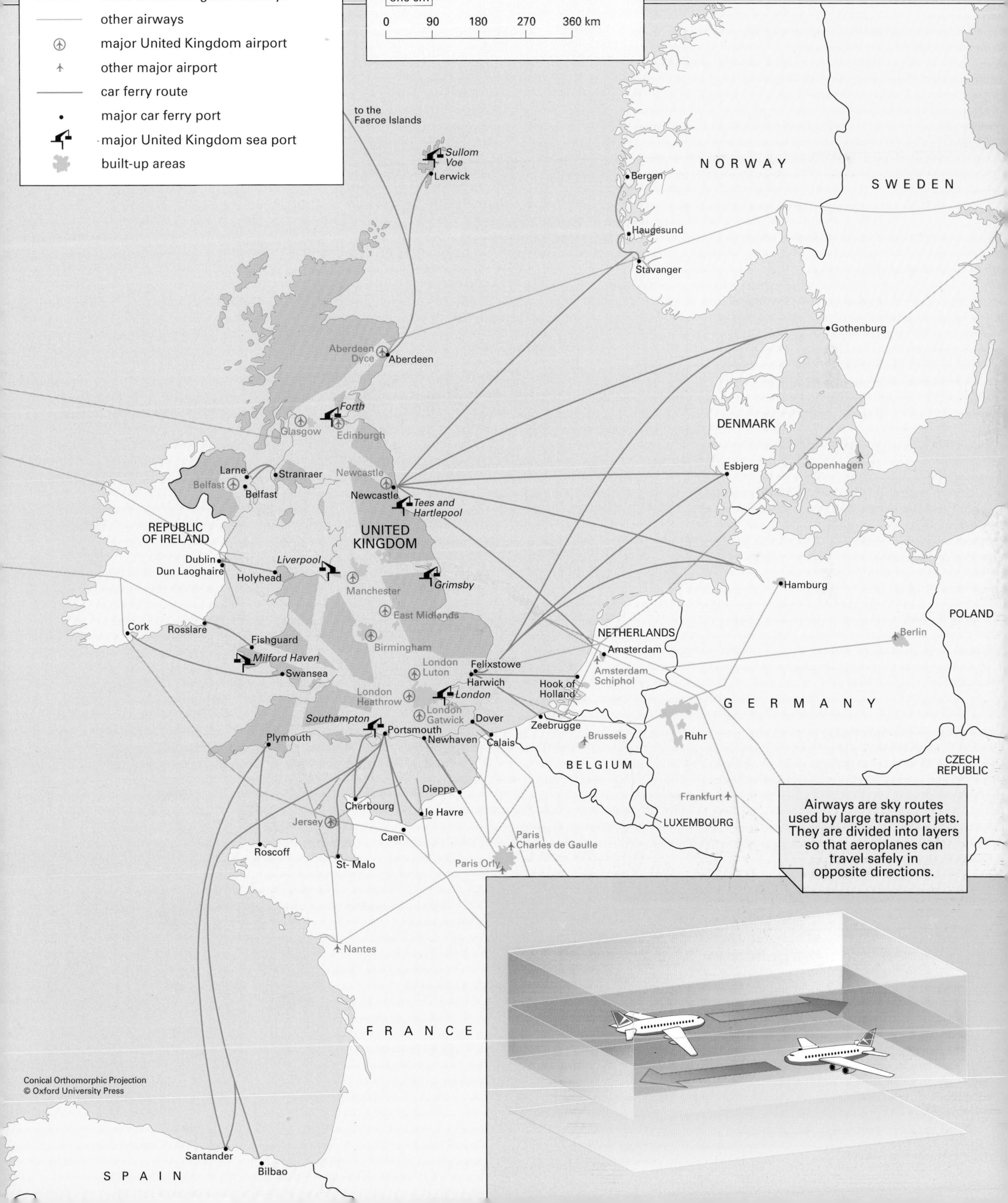

Conical Orthomorphic Projection

Airways are sky routes used by large transport jets. They are divided into layers so that aeroplanes can travel safely in opposite directions.

The United Kingdom Pollution

Damage to our land, sea, and air is called pollution.

Scale

45 km — One centimetre on the map measures 45 kilometres on the ground.

one cm

0 45 90 135 180 km

Key

built-up areas

most polluted rivers and estuaries

most polluted coasts and beaches

areas affected by acid rain

heavy pollution

moderate pollution

light pollution

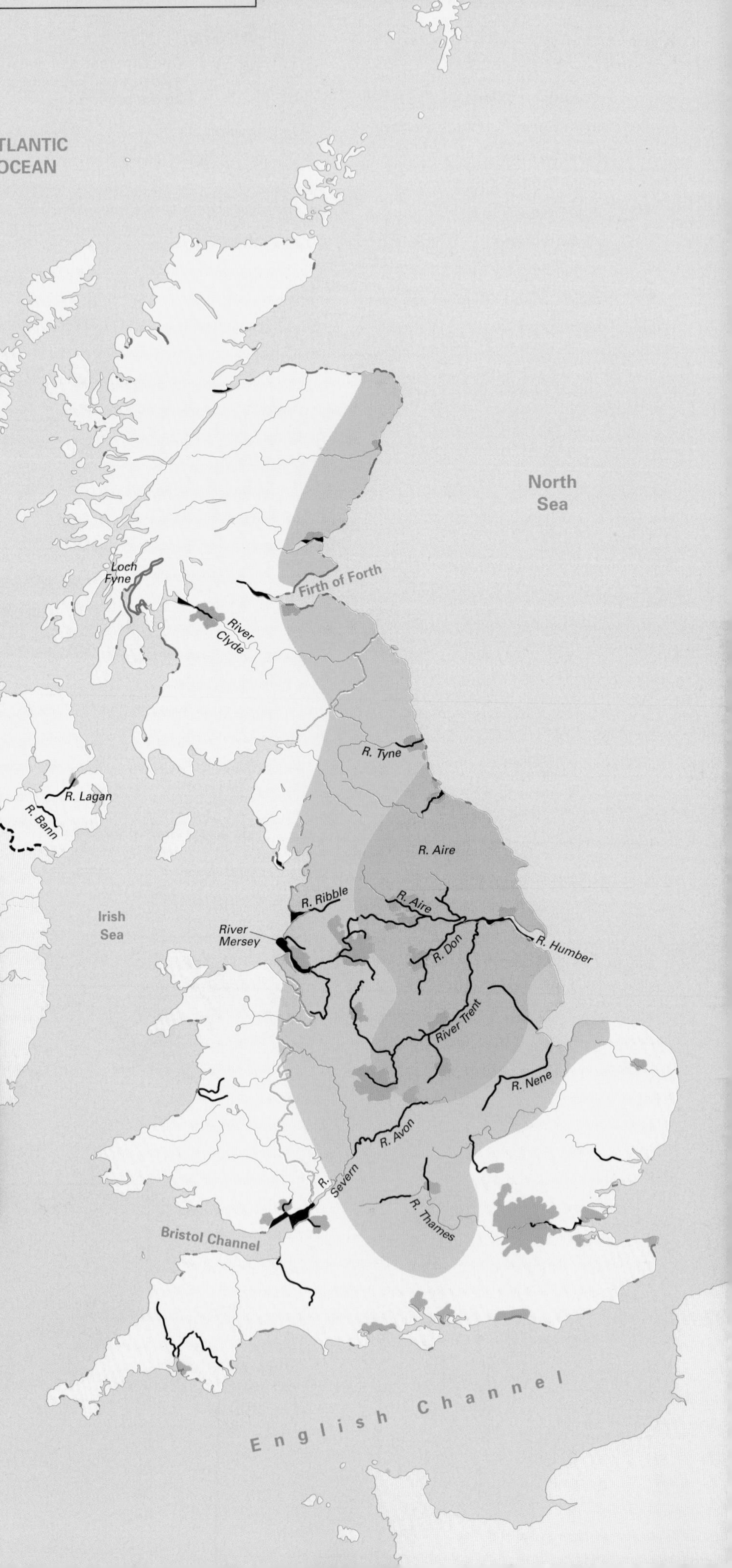

How to fight pollution

Poisonous gases from cars and factories

Poisonous waste in rivers from factories and farms

Loud noise from aircraft, factories and traffic

Dumping raw sewage in the sea

Leaving litter

STOP

Transverse Mercator Projection

The United Kingdom Conservation

Protecting nature, resources, and buildings is called conservation.

Scale

45 km — One centimetre on the map measures 45 kilometres on the ground.

one cm

0 45 90 135 180 km

Key

- National Parks
- areas of outstanding scenery and beauty
- protected coast
- ★ World Heritage Sites
- major built-up areas

National Park
Snowdonia

Area of outstanding scenery and beauty
Countryside in the Cotswold

Protected coast
The Dorset coast at Durdle Door

★ **World Heritage Site**
Stonehenge

Transverse Mercator Projection

Europe Countries

Europe is the smallest continent but is the most crowded.

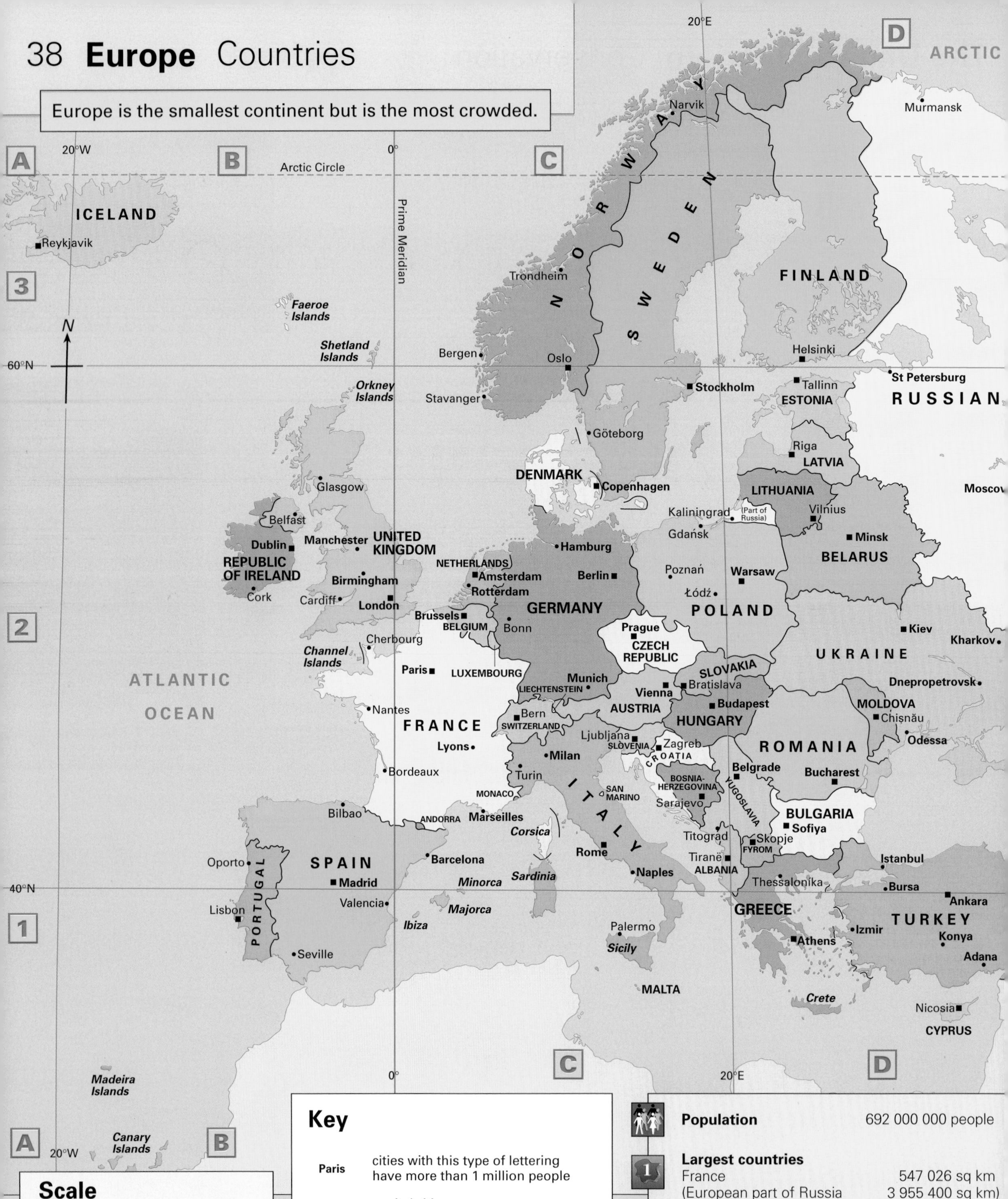

Scale

300 km — One centimetre on the map measures 300 kilometres on the ground at the Equator.

one cm

0 | 300 | 600 | 900 | 1200 km

Key

Paris	cities with this type of lettering have more than 1 million people
■	capital cities
•	other cities
ITALY	the names of countries are shown in this type of lettering
~~	country boundary

Population	692 000 000 people
Largest countries	
France	547 026 sq km
(European part of Russia	3 955 400 sq km)
Countries with the most people	
Germany	80 800 000 people
(European part of Russia	105 000 000 people)
Largest cities	
Paris (France)	9 319 000 people
Moscow (Russia)	8 801 000 people
London (UK)	6 378 000 people

Modified Gall Projection

The European Union

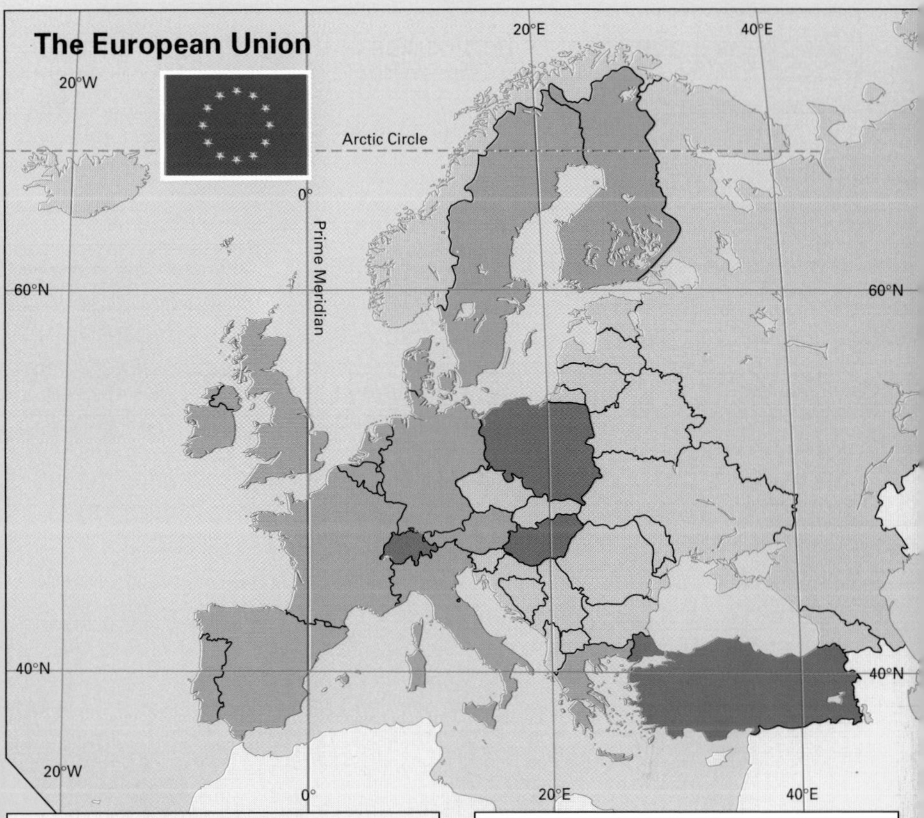

The European Union

The European Union is a group of countries which have agreed to work together and share the same plans for industry, agriculture, transport, and trade.

Key

- country boundary
- countries which are members of the European Union
- countries which have applied to be members of the European Union
- other European countries

Scale for both small maps

650 km

One centimetre on the map measures 650 kilometres on the ground at the Equator.

one cm

0 650 1300 1950 2600 km

How big is Europe?

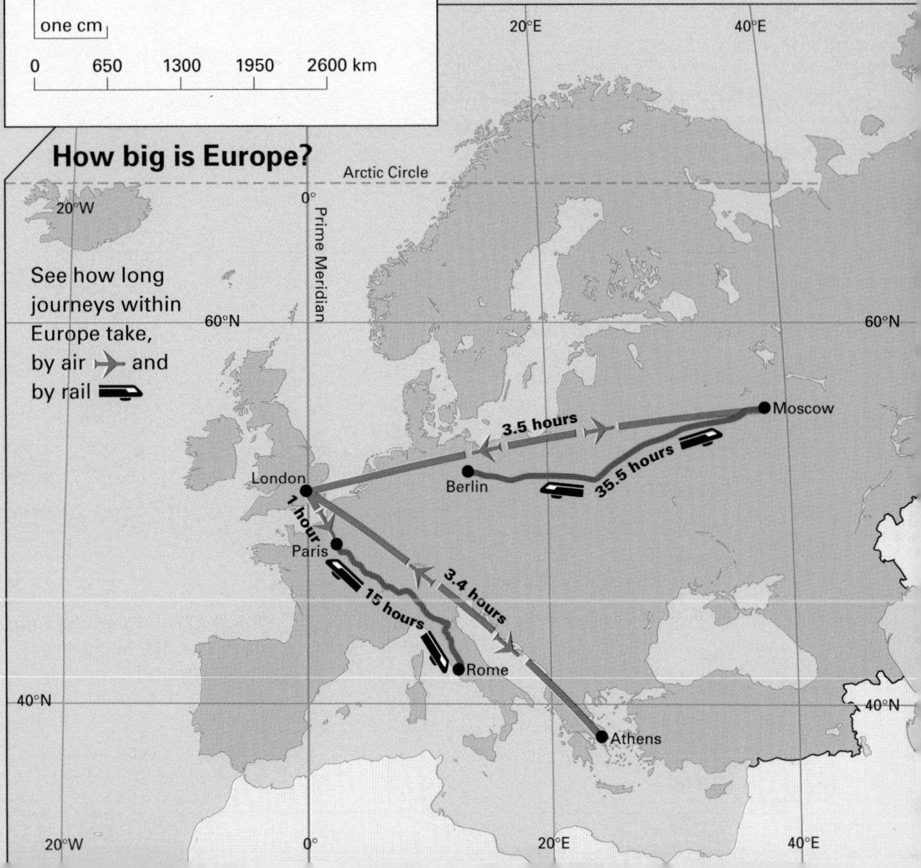

Modified Gall Projection

40 **Europe** Land height and rivers

Europe is a continent of peninsulas and islands.

Key

Colours show the height of the land.

- more than 2000 metres
- 1000 – 2000 metres
- 500 – 1000 metres
- 200 – 500 metres
- less than 200 metres
- this land is below the level of the sea
- ▲ peak or highest point
- river
- lake
- marsh
- ice cap

Scale

300 km — One centimetre on the map measures 300 kilometres on the ground.

one cm

0 300 600 900 1200 km

Area	10 498 000 sq km
Highest peak	
Mount Elbrus	5 642 m
Mont Blanc	4 807 m
Lowest point	
Caspian Sea	28 m below sea level
Largest freshwater lake	
Ladoga	18 390 sq km
Longest river	
Volga	3 688 km

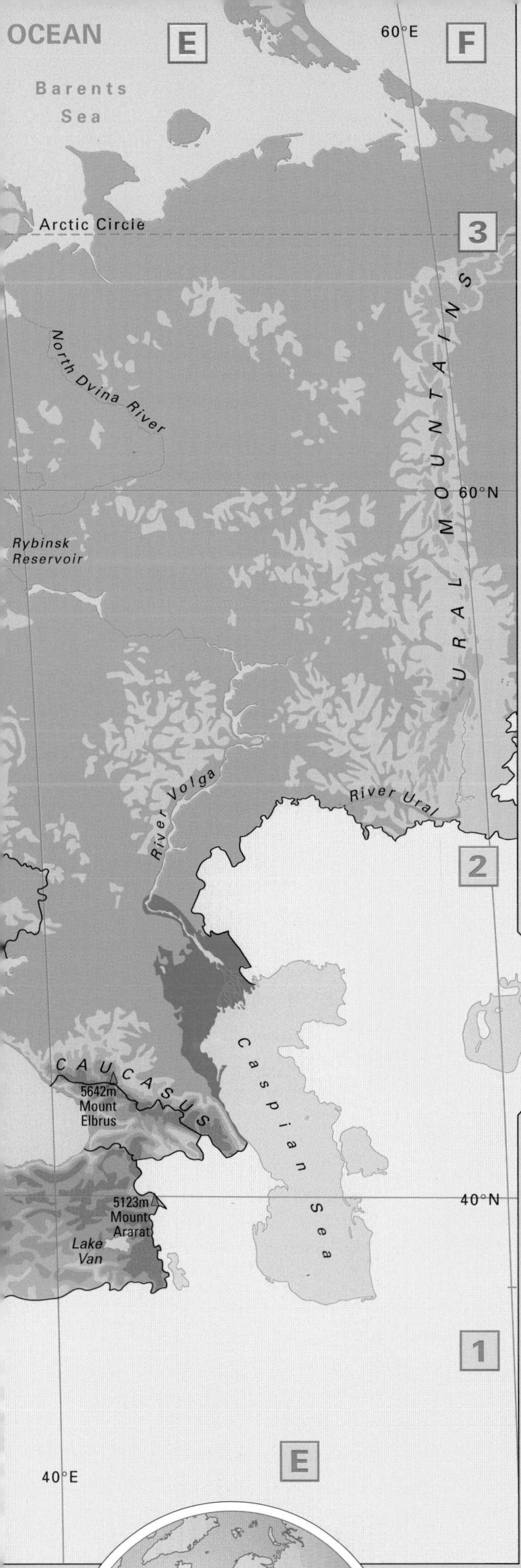

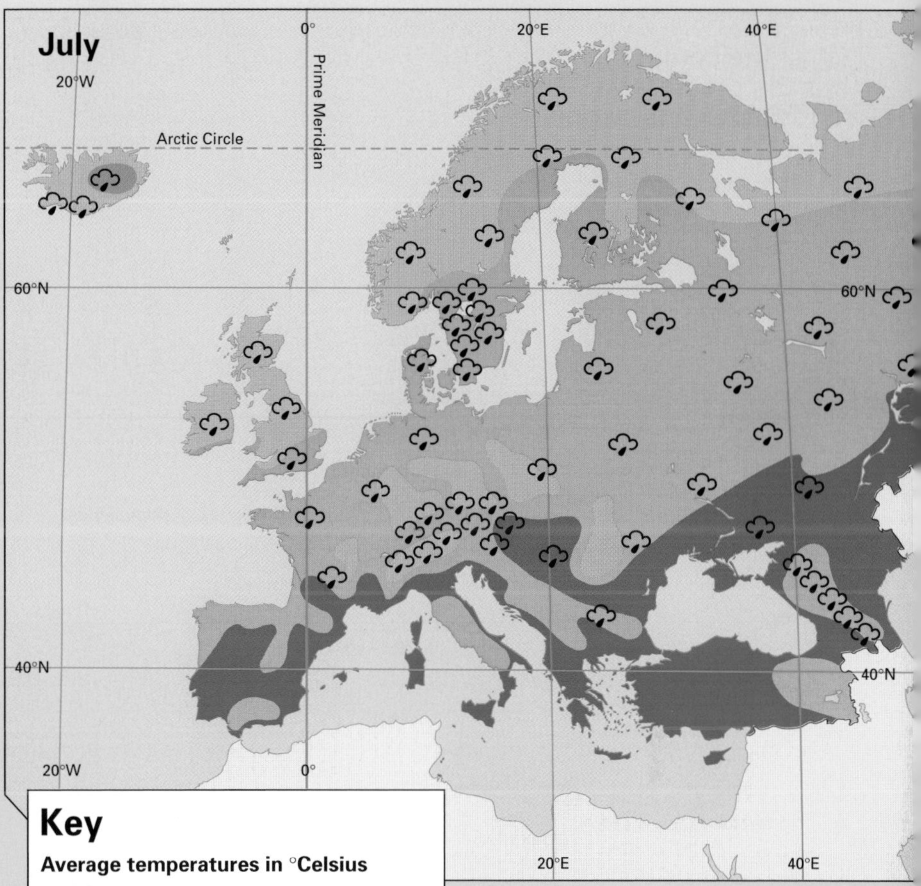

Key

Average temperatures in °Celsius

	above 20	hot
	15 - 20	warm
	5 - 15	cool
	0 - 5	cold
	below 0	very cold

Average monthly rainfall in millimetres

	over 100	very wet
	50 - 100	wet
	less than 50	dry

Scale

650 km — One centimetre on the map measures 650 kilometres on the ground.

one cm

0 650 1300 1950 2600 km

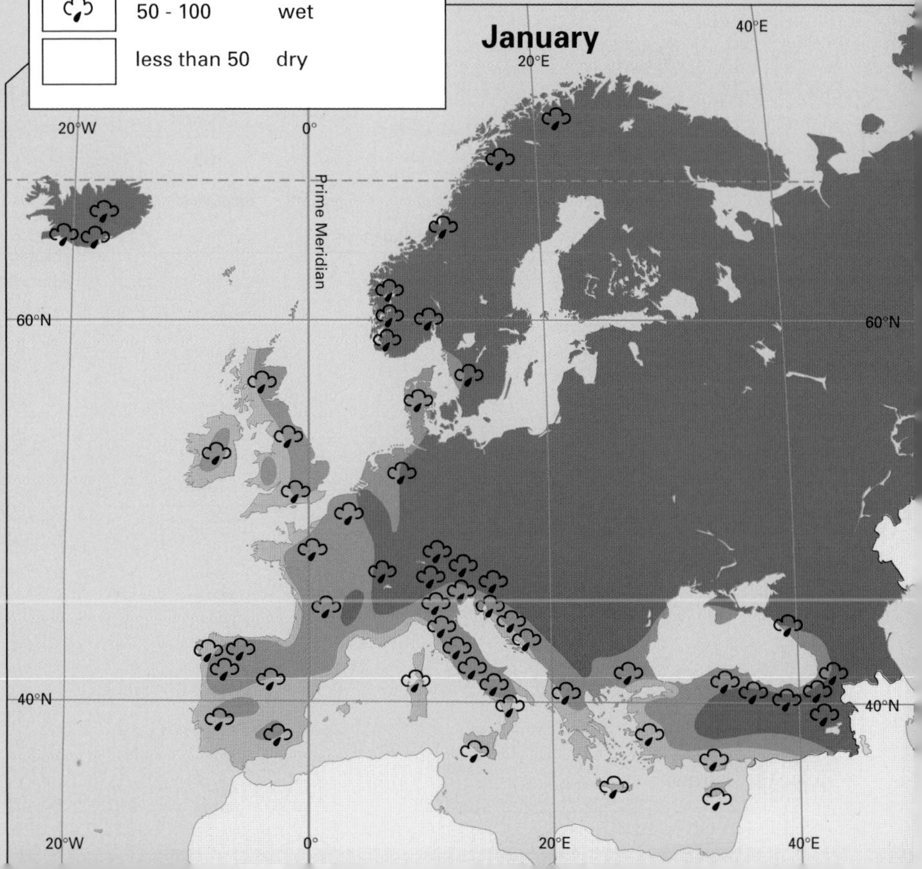

Of all the continents, Asia has the greatest variety of landscapes and people.

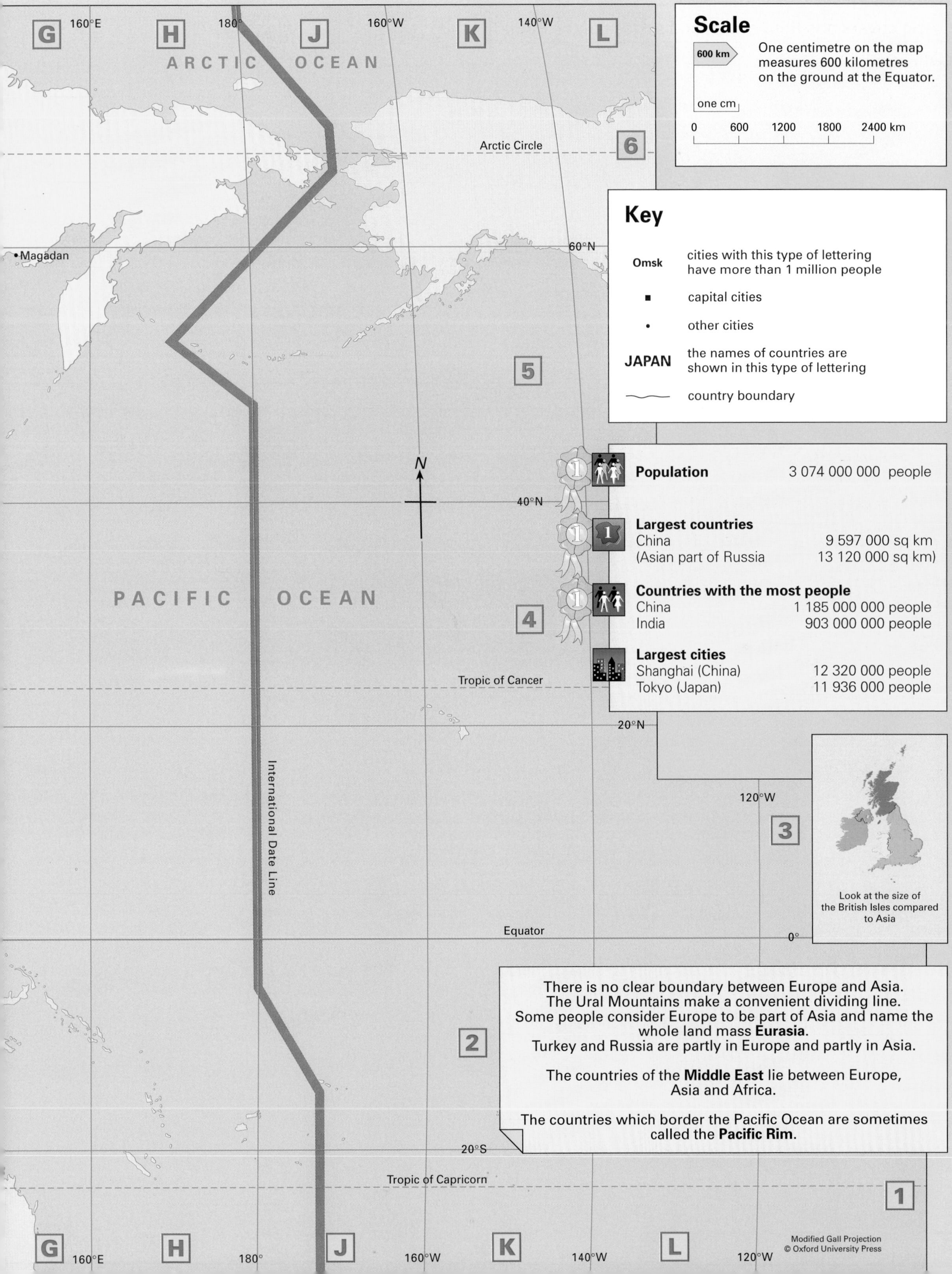

Scale

600 km | one cm

One centimetre on the map measures 600 kilometres on the ground at the Equator.

0 600 1200 1800 2400 km

Key

Omsk	cities with this type of lettering have more than 1 million people
■	capital cities
•	other cities
JAPAN	the names of countries are shown in this type of lettering
~~	country boundary

Population	3 074 000 000 people
Largest countries	
China	9 597 000 sq km
(Asian part of Russia	13 120 000 sq km)
Countries with the most people	
China	1 185 000 000 people
India	903 000 000 people
Largest cities	
Shanghai (China)	12 320 000 people
Tokyo (Japan)	11 936 000 people

There is no clear boundary between Europe and Asia. The Ural Mountains make a convenient dividing line. Some people consider Europe to be part of Asia and name the whole land mass **Eurasia**. Turkey and Russia are partly in Europe and partly in Asia.

The countries of the **Middle East** lie between Europe, Asia and Africa.

The countries which border the Pacific Ocean are sometimes called the **Pacific Rim**.

Modified Gall Projection

Asia Land height and rivers

Asia covers one third of the land surface of the Earth.

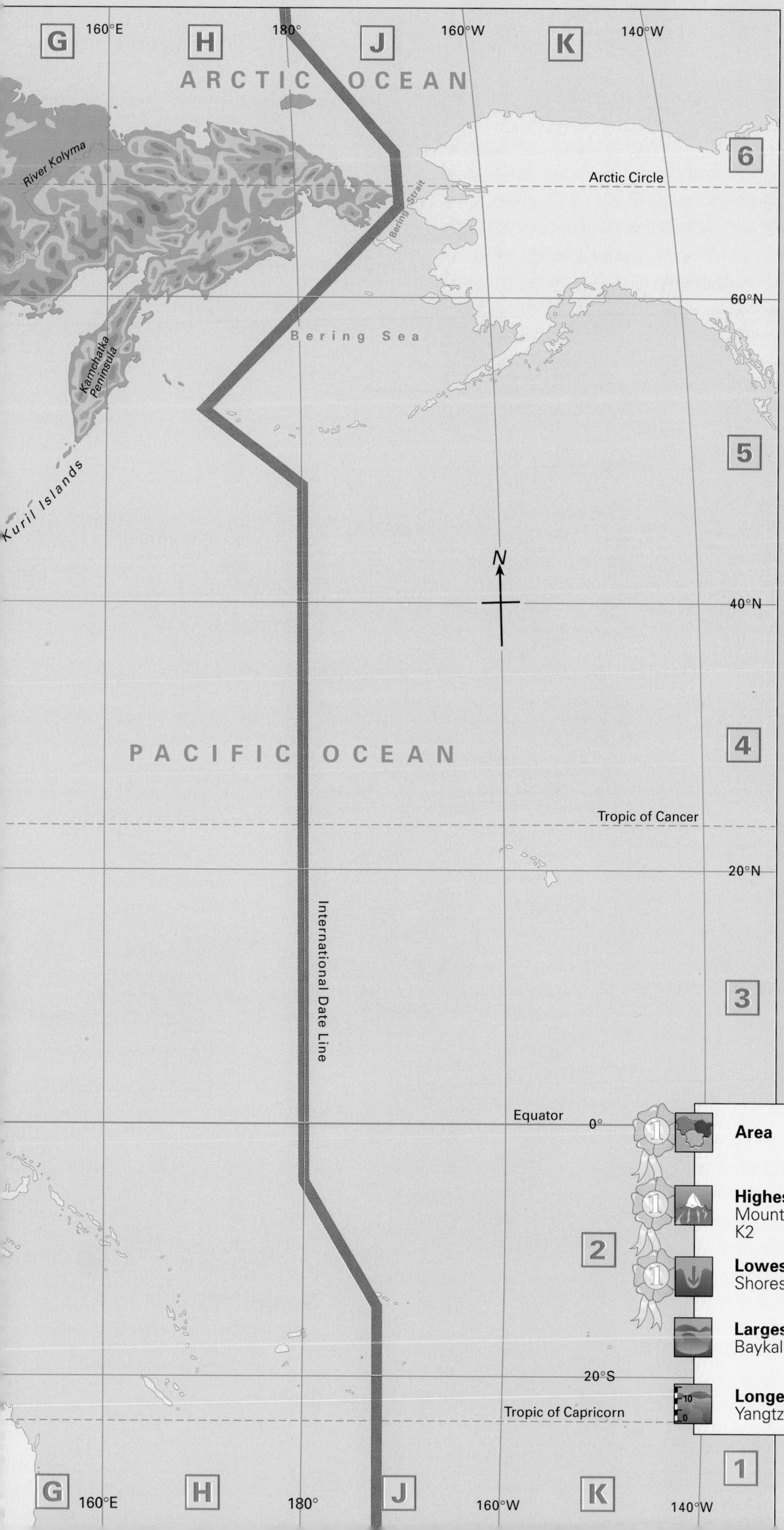

Scale

600 km

one cm

One centimetre on the map measures 600 kilometres on the ground at the Equator.

0 600 1200 1800 2400 km

Key

Colours show the height of the land.

- more than 5000 metres
- 2000 – 5000 metres
- 1000 – 2000 metres
- 500 – 1000 metres
- 200 – 500 metres
- less than 200 metres
- this land is below the level of the sea
- peak or highest point
- river
- lake
- marsh
- desert
- ice cap

Area	44 387 000 sq km
Highest peaks	
Mount Everest	8 848 m
K2	8 611 m
Lowest point	
Shores of the Dead Sea	395 m below sea level
Largest freshwater lake	
Baykal	30 500 sq km
Longest river	
Yangtze	6 380 km

Modified Gall Projection

Many countries in Africa have no sea coast.

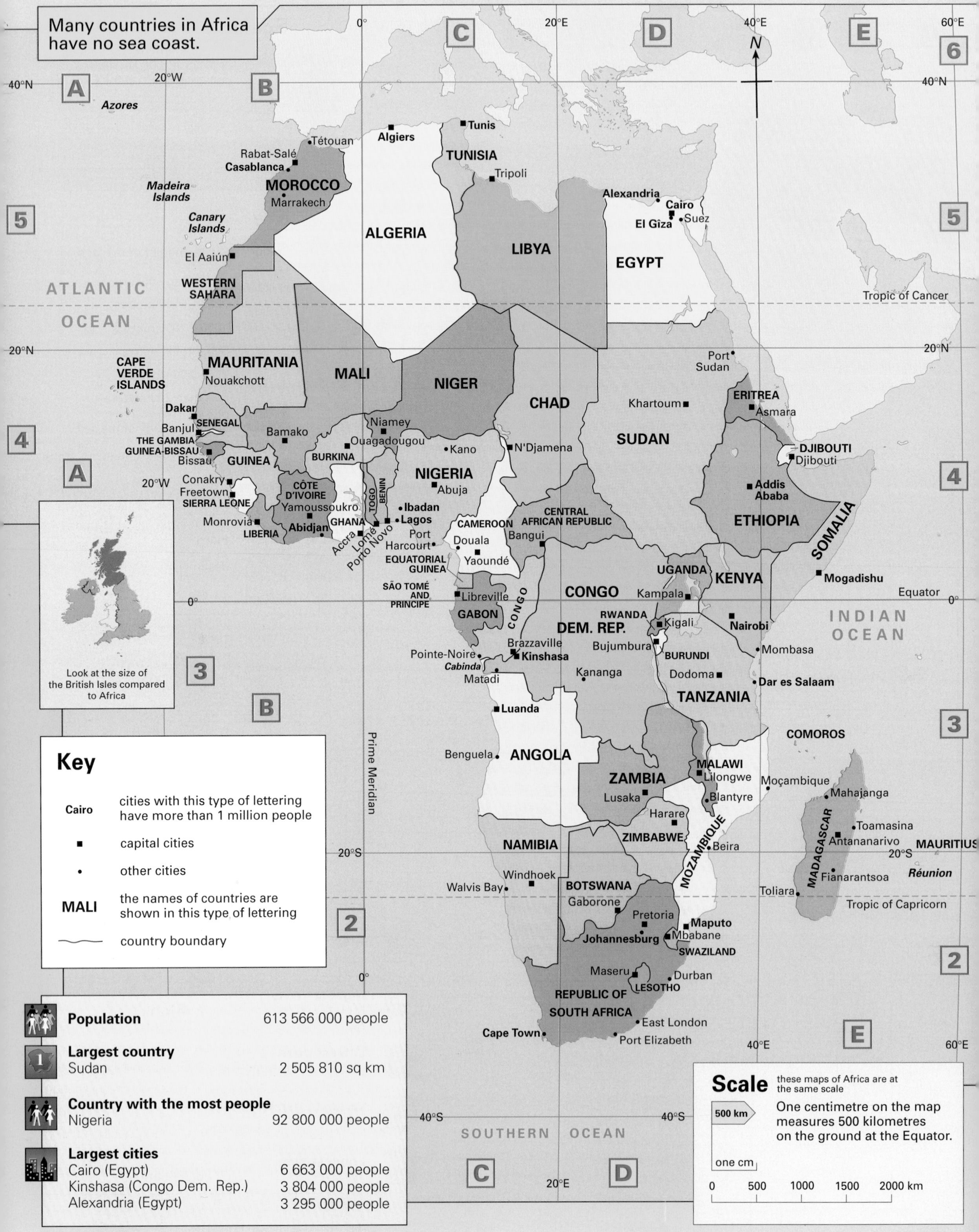

Look at the size of the British Isles compared to Africa

Key

Cairo	cities with this type of lettering have more than 1 million people
■	capital cities
•	other cities
MALI	the names of countries are shown in this type of lettering
~	country boundary

Population	613 566 000 people
Largest country Sudan	2 505 810 sq km
Country with the most people Nigeria	92 800 000 people
Largest cities	
Cairo (Egypt)	6 663 000 people
Kinshasa (Congo Dem. Rep.)	3 804 000 people
Alexandria (Egypt)	3 295 000 people

Scale these maps of Africa are at the same scale

500 km — one cm

One centimetre on the map measures 500 kilometres on the ground at the Equator.

0 500 1000 1500 2000 km

Modified Gall Projection

Almost all of Africa is warm or hot.

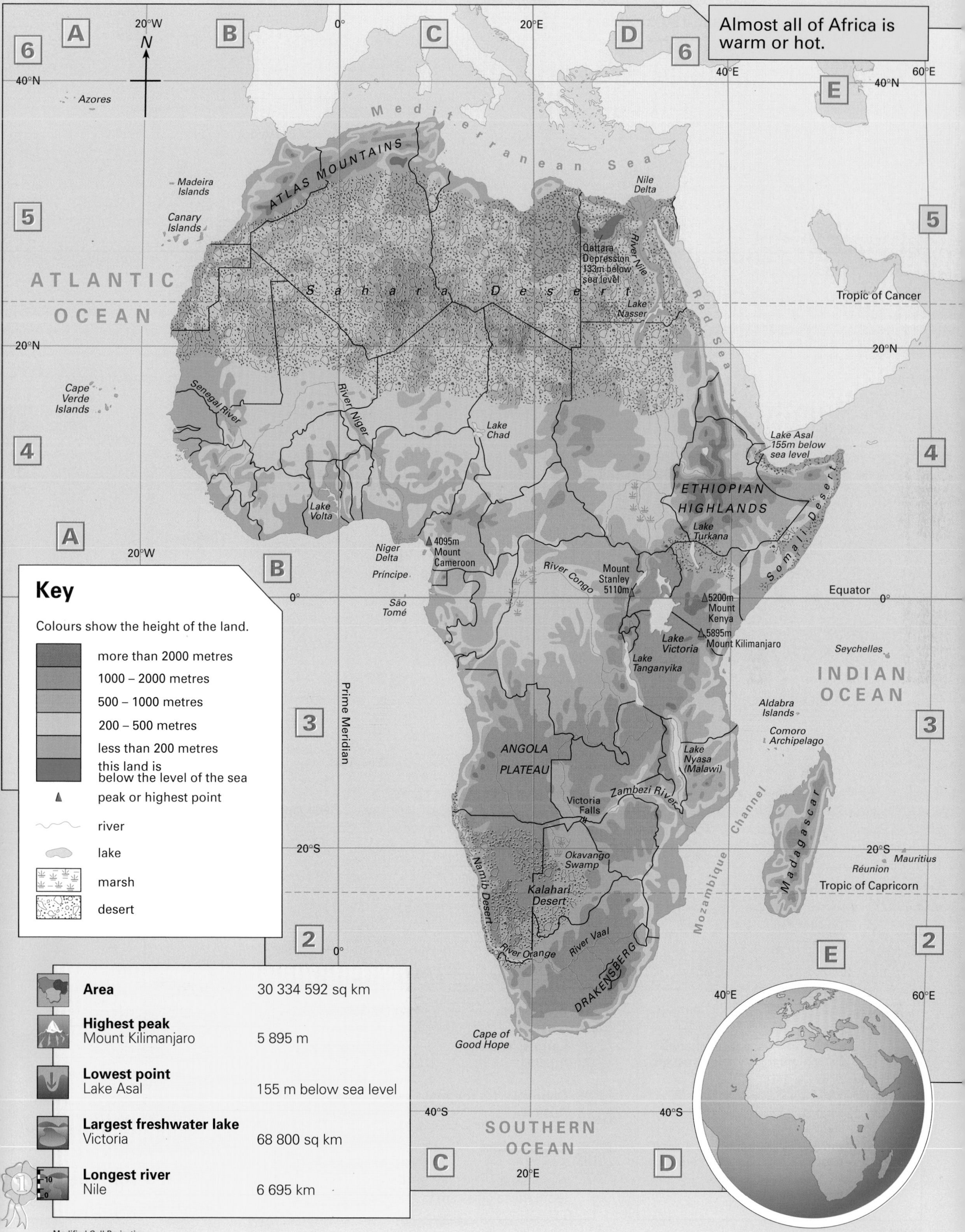

Key

Colours show the height of the land.

- more than 2000 metres
- 1000 – 2000 metres
- 500 – 1000 metres
- 200 – 500 metres
- less than 200 metres
- this land is below the level of the sea
- peak or highest point
- river
- lake
- marsh
- desert

Area	30 334 592 sq km
Highest peak Mount Kilimanjaro	5 895 m
Lowest point Lake Asal	155 m below sea level
Largest freshwater lake Victoria	68 800 sq km
Longest river Nile	6 695 km

Modified Gall Projection

Oceania is sometimes called Australasia.

Look at the size of the British Isles compared to Oceania

Key

Sydney	cities with this type of lettering have more than 1 million people
■	capital cities
•	other cities
FIJI	the names of countries are shown in this type of lettering
~	country boundary

Population	25 800 000 people
Largest country Australia	7 686 850 sq km
Country with the most people Australia	17 800 000 people
Largest cities Sydney Melbourne (both these cities are in Australia)	 3 714 000 people 3 189 000 people

Scale

these maps of Oceania are at the same scale

500 km — one cm

One centimetre on the map measures 500 kilometres on the ground at the Equator.

0 500 1000 1500 2000 km

Modified Gall Projection

There are about ten thousand islands spread over a vast area of the central and southern Pacific Ocean.

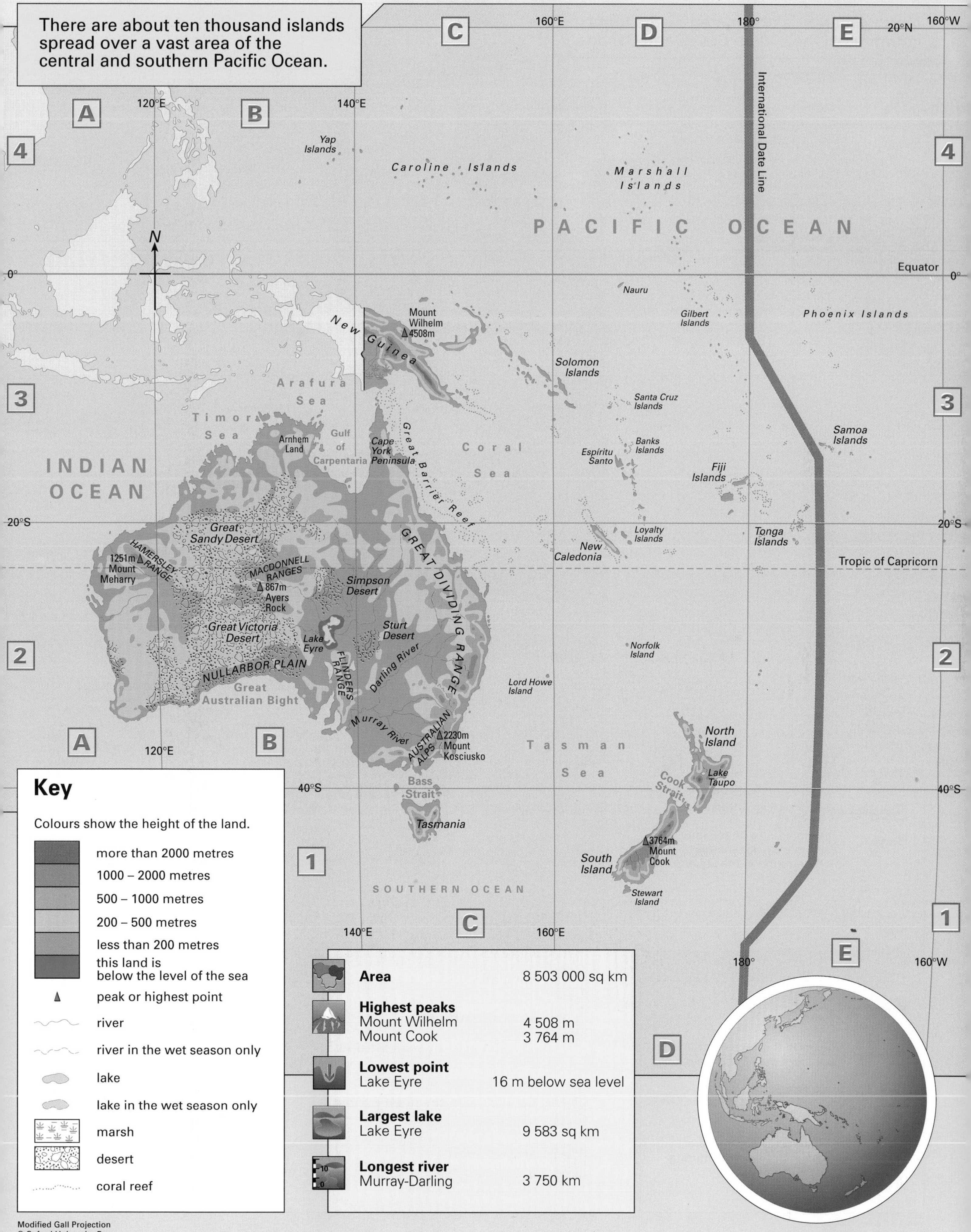

Key

Colours show the height of the land.

- more than 2000 metres
- 1000 – 2000 metres
- 500 – 1000 metres
- 200 – 500 metres
- less than 200 metres
- this land is below the level of the sea
- peak or highest point
- river
- river in the wet season only
- lake
- lake in the wet season only
- marsh
- desert
- coral reef

Area	8 503 000 sq km
Highest peaks	
Mount Wilhelm	4 508 m
Mount Cook	3 764 m
Lowest point	
Lake Eyre	16 m below sea level
Largest lake	
Lake Eyre	9 583 sq km
Longest river	
Murray-Darling	3 750 km

Modified Gall Projection

North America Countries

North America is dominated by the huge countries of the United States and Canada.

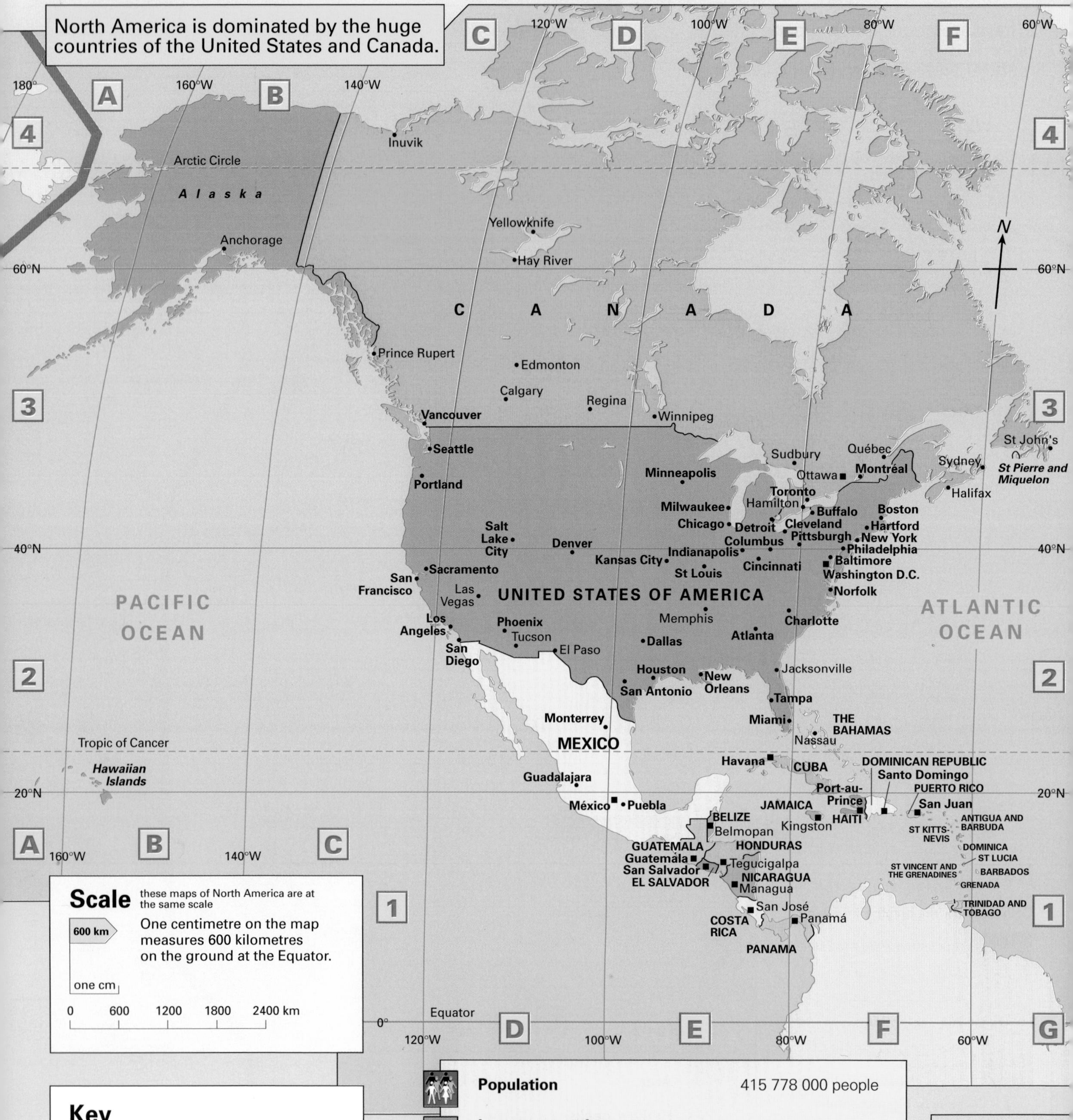

Scale these maps of North America are at the same scale

600 km

One centimetre on the map measures 600 kilometres on the ground at the Equator.

one cm

0 600 1200 1800 2400 km

Key

Miami	cities with this type of lettering have more than 1 million people
■	capital cities
•	other cities
CUBA	the names of countries are shown in this type of lettering
~	country boundary

Population 415 778 000 people

Largest countries
Canada 9 976 140 sq km
United States of America (USA) 9 372 610 sq km
(The world's longest border is between the United States and Canada.)

Country with the most people
United States of America 257 000 000 people

Largest cities
Mexico (Mexico) 15 048 000 people
New York City (USA) 7 333 253 people

Look at the size of the British Isles compared to North America

Modified Gall Projection

The huge Rocky Mountain range forms the backbone of North America.

Key

Colours show the height of the land.

- more than 2000 metres
- 1000 – 2000 metres
- 500 – 1000 metres
- 200 – 500 metres
- less than 200 metres
- this land is below the level of the sea
- peak or highest point
- river
- lake
- marsh
- desert
- ice cap

Area	24 241 000 sq km
Highest peak Mount McKinley	6 194 m
Lowest point Death Valley	86 m below sea level
Largest freshwater lake Lake Superior	83 270 sq km
Longest river Mississippi-Missouri	6019 km

Modified Gall Projection

Brazilians speak Portuguese. Most other South Americans speak Spanish.

Scale

these maps of South America are at the same scale

500 km

One centimetre on the map measures 500 kilometres on the ground at the Equator.

one cm

0 500 1000 1500 2000 km

Key

Lima — cities with this type of lettering have more than 1 million people

■ — capital cities

• — other cities

PERU — the names of countries are shown in this type of lettering

— country boundary

Population	283 519 000 people
Largest countries	
Brazil	8 511 966 sq km
Argentina	2 776 890 sq km
Country with most people	
Brazil	159 100 000 people
Largest cities	
Buenos Aires (Argentina)	11 256 000 people
São Paulo (Brazil)	9 627 000 people
Rio de Janeiro (Brazil)	5 473 000 people

Modified Gall Projection

Key

Colours show the height of the land.

- more than 5000 metres
- 2000 – 5000 metres
- 1000 – 2000 metres
- 500 – 1000 metres
- 200 – 500 metres
- less than 200 metres
- this land is below the level of the sea
- peak or highest point
- river
- lake
- marsh
- desert
- ice cap

Area	17 832 000 sq km
Highest peaks	
Mount Aconcagua	6 960 m
Ojos del Salado	6 908 m
Lowest point	
Valdés Peninsula	40 m below sea level
Largest freshwater lake	
Titicaca	8 340 sq km
Longest river	
Amazon	6 516 km
World's highest waterfall	
Angel Falls (Venezuela)	979 m

Modified Gall Projection

Antarctica

Antarctica has 90% of all of the ice in the world.

Scale

340 km — One centimetre on the map measures 340 kilometres on the ground.

one cm

0 340 680 1020 1360 km

Look at the size of the British Isles compared to Antarctica

Area 13 340 000 sq km

Highest point
Vinson Massif 5 140 m

World's longest glacier
Lambert Glacier 400 km

the South Pole

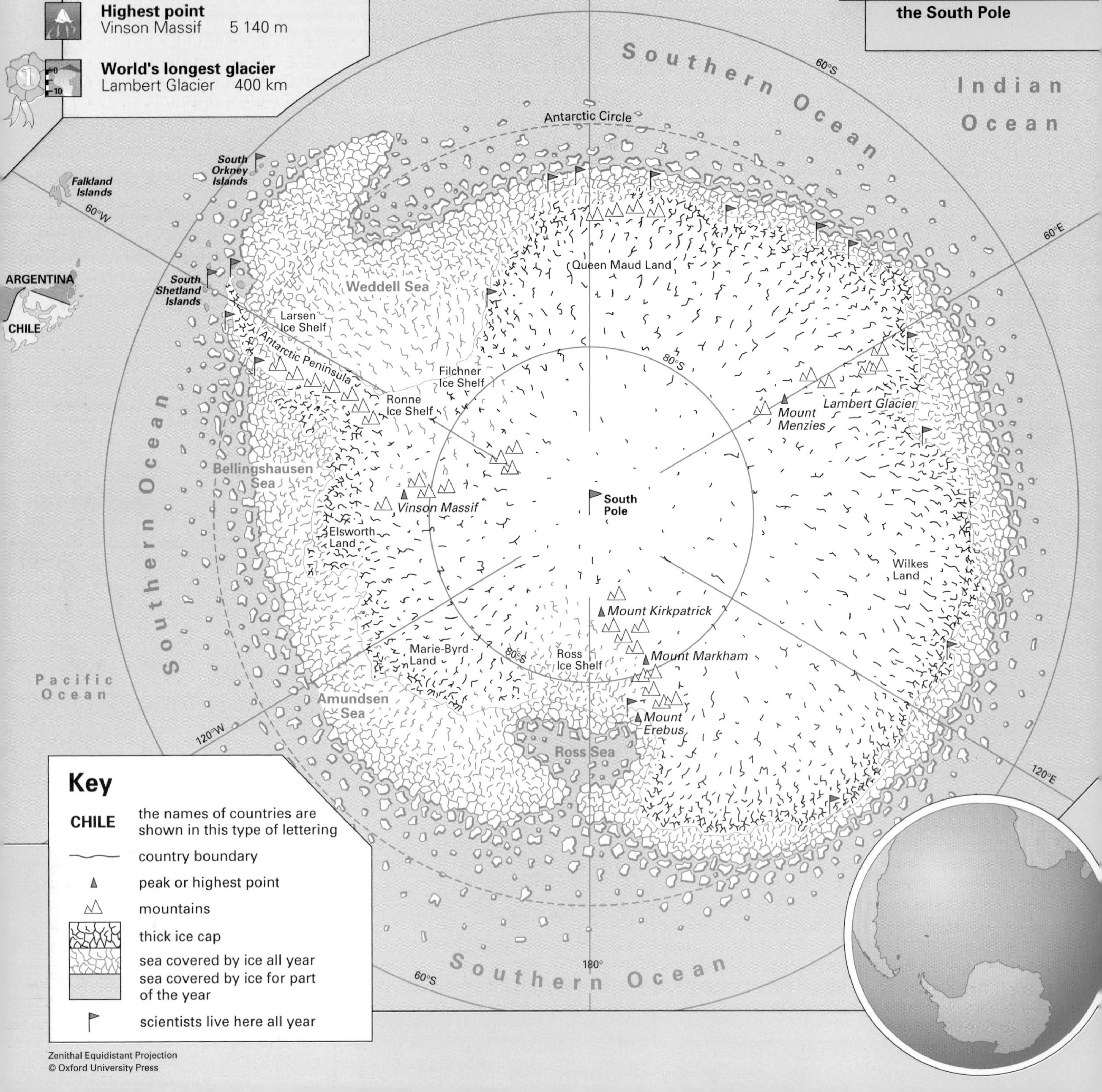

Key

CHILE	the names of countries are shown in this type of lettering
	country boundary
	peak or highest point
	mountains
	thick ice cap
	sea covered by ice all year
	sea covered by ice for part of the year
	scientists live here all year

Zenithal Equidistant Projection

The Arctic Ocean

Most of the Arctic is a huge frozen ocean.

the North Pole

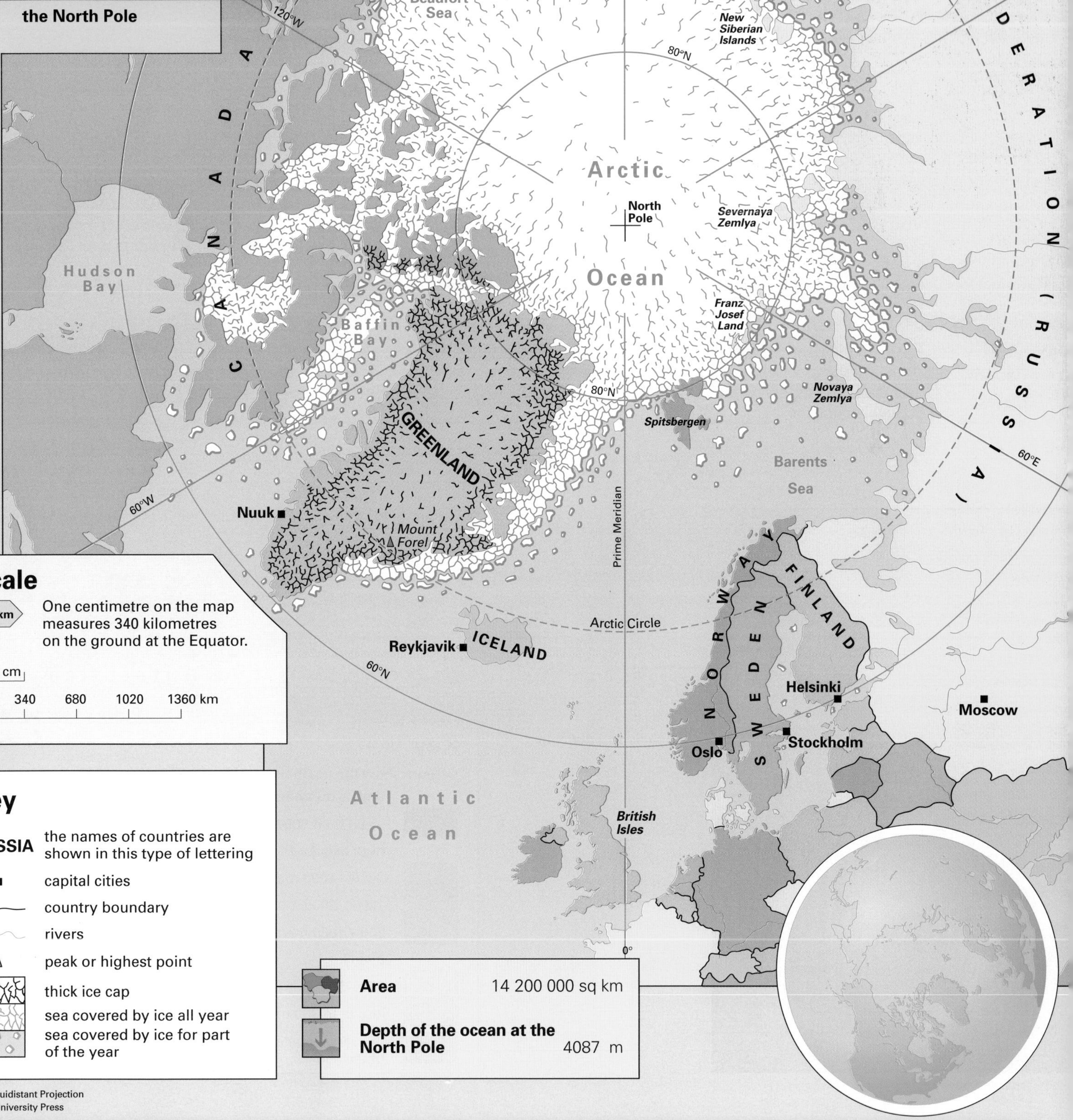

Scale

340 km

One centimetre on the map measures 340 kilometres on the ground at the Equator.

one cm

0 | 340 | 680 | 1020 | 1360 km

Key

RUSSIA the names of countries are shown in this type of lettering

■ capital cities

country boundary

rivers

peak or highest point

thick ice cap

sea covered by ice all year

sea covered by ice for part of the year

Area 14 200 000 sq km

Depth of the ocean at the North Pole 4087 m

Zenithal Equidistant Projection

Two-thirds of the surface of the earth is covered with water. The rest is land.

Scale

1050 km

One centimetre on the map measures 1050 kilometres on the ground at the Equator.

one cm

0 1050 2100 3150 4200 km

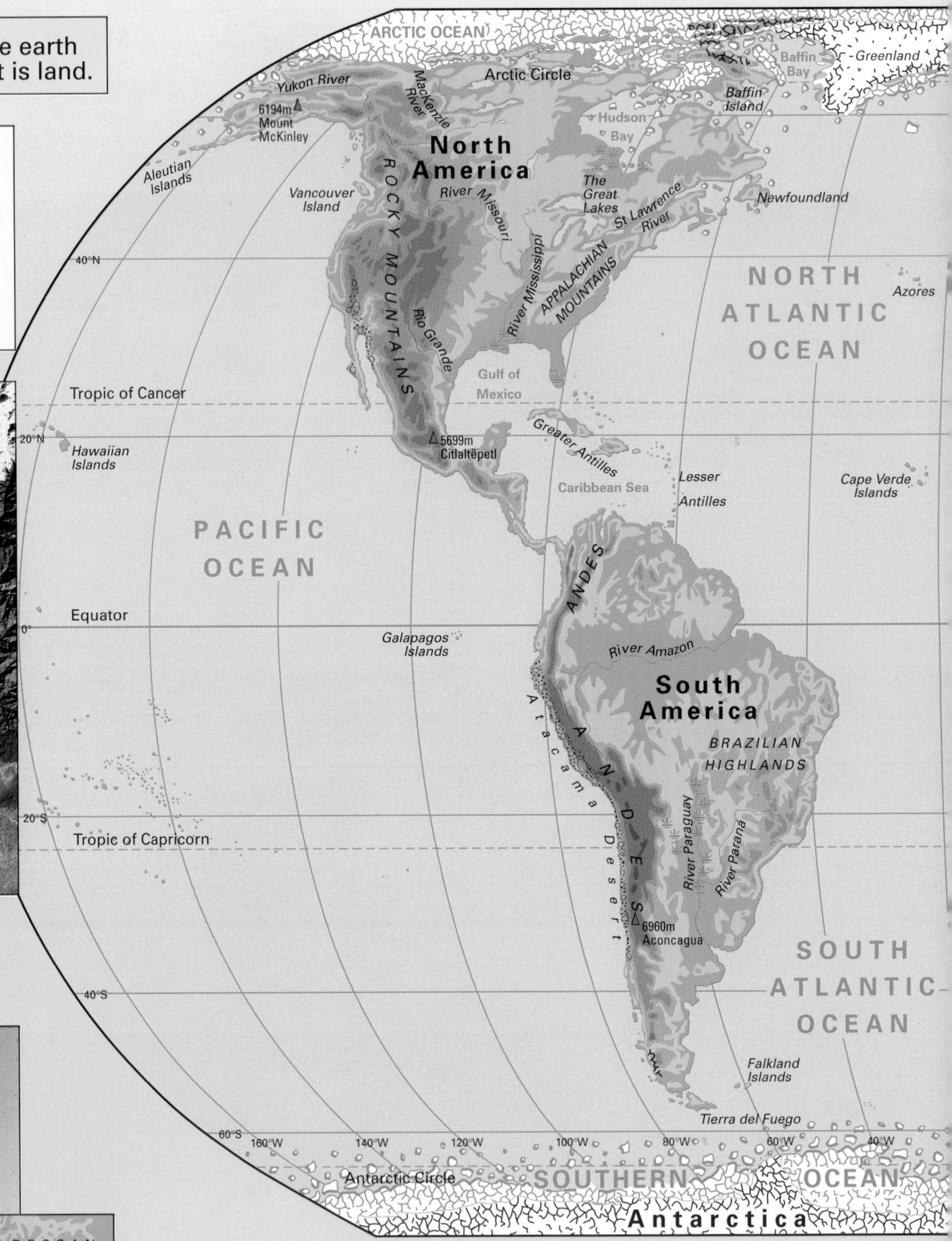

high mountains
The Himalayas seen from space

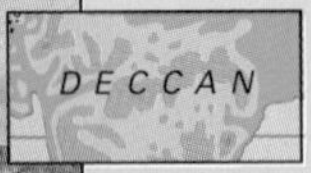

high hills and plateaux
Deccan, India

Key

Colours show the height of the land

high mountains
- more than 5000 metres

high hills and plateaux
- 2000 – 5000 metres
- 1000 – 2000 metres
- 500 – 1000 metres

plains
- 200 – 500 metres
- less than 200 metres
- this land is below the level of the sea

- peak or highest point
- river
- lake
- marsh
- desert
- ice on land
- ice on sea

Eckert IV Projection

ARCTIC OCEAN
Barents Sea
Iceland
North Sea
British Isles
Europe
R. Rhine
River Danube
4807m Mont Blanc
ALPS
Pripet Marshes
River Volga
Mount Elbrus 5642m
CAUCASUS
Black Sea
TAURUS MOUNTAINS
Mediterranean Sea
ATLAS MOUNTAINS
Canary Islands
Sahara Desert
River Nile
Red Sea
River Niger
Lake Chad
Africa
River Congo
Lake Victoria
5895m Mount Kilimanjaro
Lake Tanganyika
Lake Nyasa (Malawi)
River Zambezi
Namib Desert
Okavango Swamp
Kalahari Desert
Madagascar
Seychelles
URAL MOUNTAINS
Yenisey River
River Ob
River Irtysh
Aral Sea
Caspian Sea
ZAGROS MOUNTAINS
Communism Peak 7495m
8611m K2
TIBETAN PLATEAU
HIMALAYAS
8848m Mount Everest
River Ganges
DECCAN
Arabian Sea
Bay of Bengal
ALTAI MOUNTAINS
Asia
Gobi Desert
River Lena
Lake Baykal
Hwang-Ho River
River Yangtze
Mekong River
Arctic Circle
Sea of Okhotsk
Bering Sea
60°N
Honshu
40°N
East China Sea
Tropic of Cancer
PACIFIC OCEAN
20°N
South China Sea
Philippines
Caroline Islands
Marshall Islands
Borneo
Sumatra
Java
Equator
0°
New Guinea
4508m Mount Wilhelm
Solomon Islands
INDIAN OCEAN
Oceania
Fiji Islands
Great Sandy Desert
Great Victoria Desert
NULLARBOR PLAIN
River Darling
GREAT DIVIDING RANGE
Murray R.
New Caledonia
20°S
Tropic of Capricorn
North Island
Tasman Sea
40°S
Tasmania
South Island
3764m Mount Cook
160°E
180°
SOUTH ATLANTIC OCEAN
Prime Meridian
SOUTHERN OCEAN
20°W
0°
20°E
40°E
60°E
80°E
100°E
120°E
140°E
Antarctica

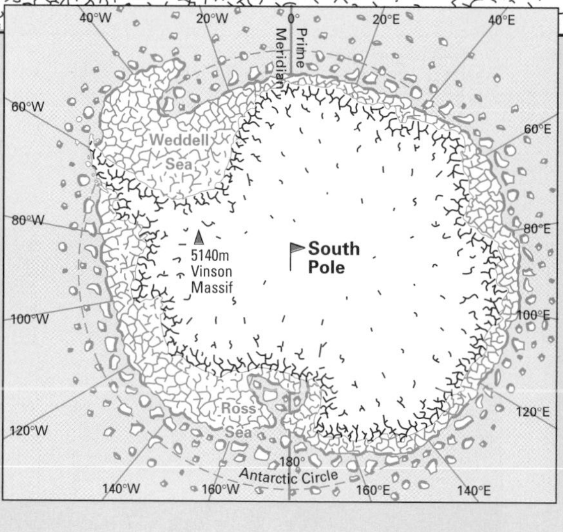
40°W
20°W
0°
Prime Meridian
20°E
40°E
60°W
60°E
Weddell Sea
80°W
80°E
5140m Vinson Massif
South Pole
100°W
100°E
Ross Sea
120°W
120°E
180°
Antarctic Circle
140°W
160°W
160°E
140°E

River Amazon

plains
The basin of the River Amazon, Brazil

Patterns of temperature and rainfall throughout the year make types of climate.

Scale

1050 km

One centimetre on the map measures 1050 kilometres on the ground at the Equator.

one cm

0 | 1050 | 2100 | 3150 | 4200 km

Key

- polar climate
- continental climate
- coastal climate
- Mediterranean climate
- desert climate
- tropical climate
- equatorial climate
- high mountain climate
- * places with record breaking climates

Eckert IV Projection

Hottest place
Al' Aziziyah (Libya)

Coldest place
Vostok (Antarctica)

Driest place
Arica, Atacama Desert (Chile)

Wettest place
Mount Waialeale (Hawaii)

Windiest place
Mount Washington (USA)

Snowiest place
Mount Ranier (USA)

polar climate
very cold all year

continental climate
very cold winters, warmer summers

coastal climate
warm summers, mild winters, rain all year

Mediterranean climate
hot dry summers, warm wet winters

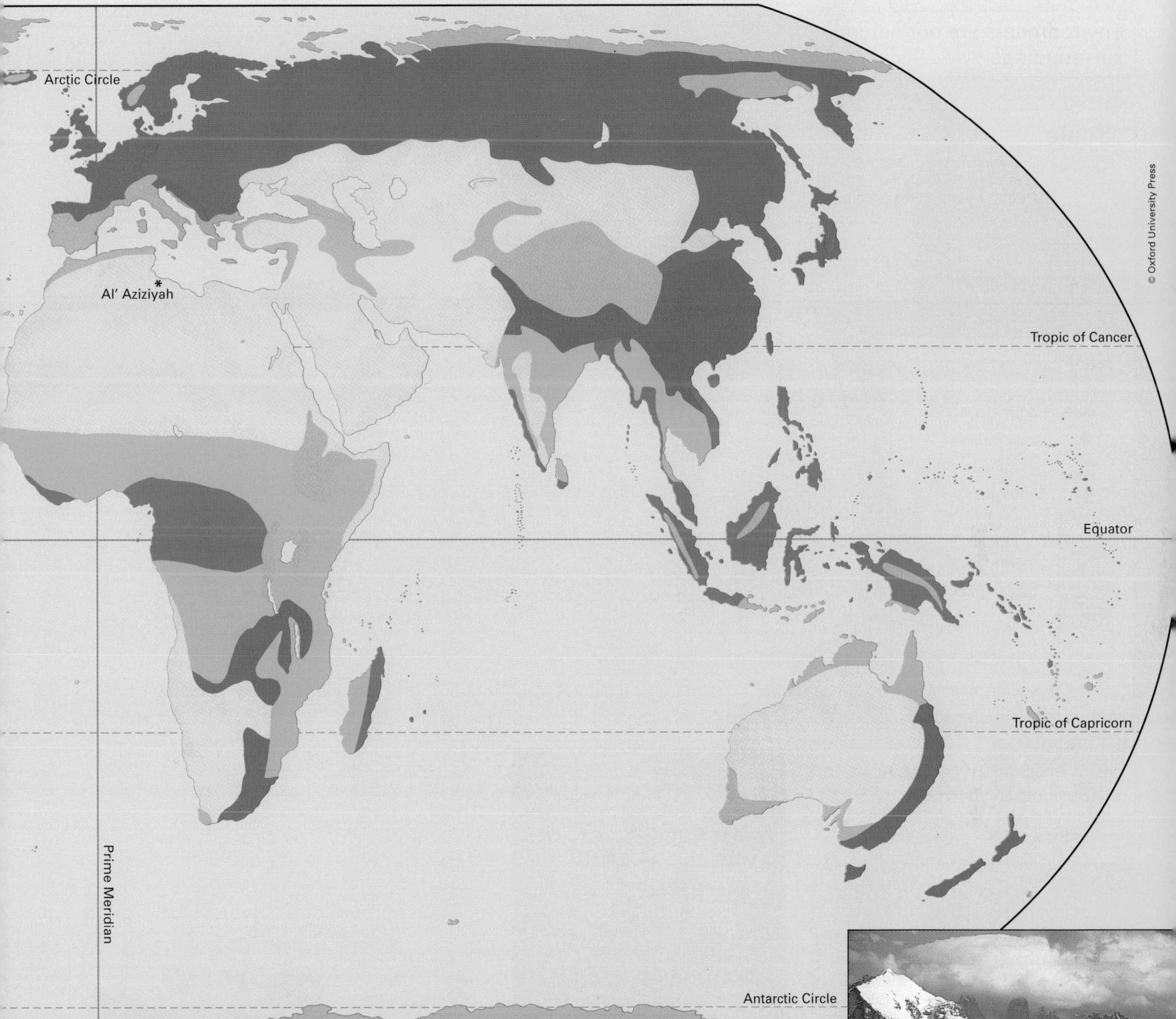

high mountain climate
becomes colder with height

tropical climate
very hot all year with a wet season and a dry season

equatorial climate
very hot and wet all year

desert climate
very dry all year

Environments are our natural surroundings.

Scale

1050 km — one cm

One centimetre on the map measures 1050 kilometres on the ground at the Equator.

0 — 1050 — 2100 — 3150 — 4200 km

Key

- high mountains
- cold forest
- savannah
- hot forest
- desert
- marsh
- ice on land
- ice on the sea
- very large built up areas
- country boundary

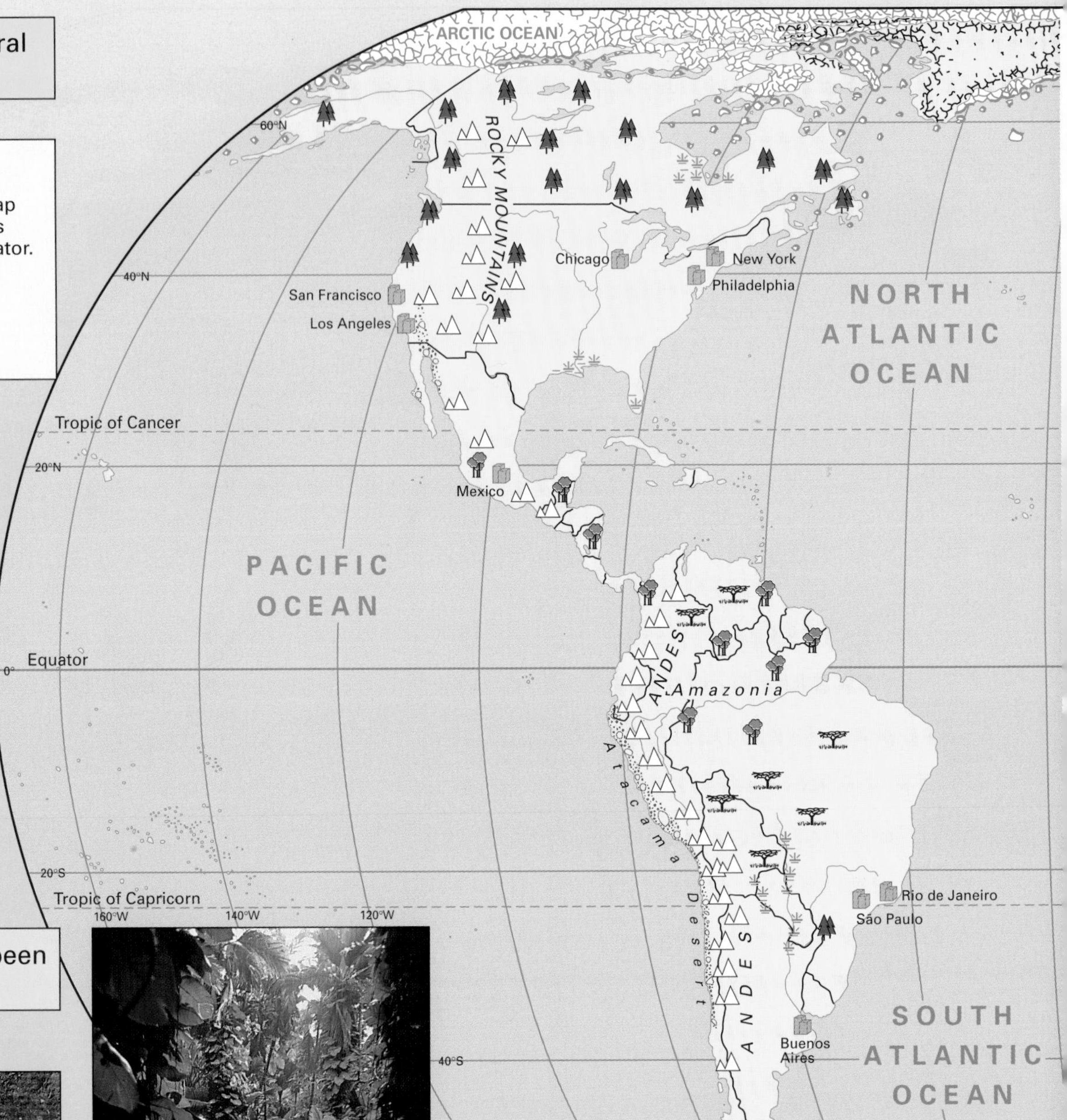

Most environments have been influenced by people.

hot forest

very large built up area

savannah

cold forest

desert

marsh

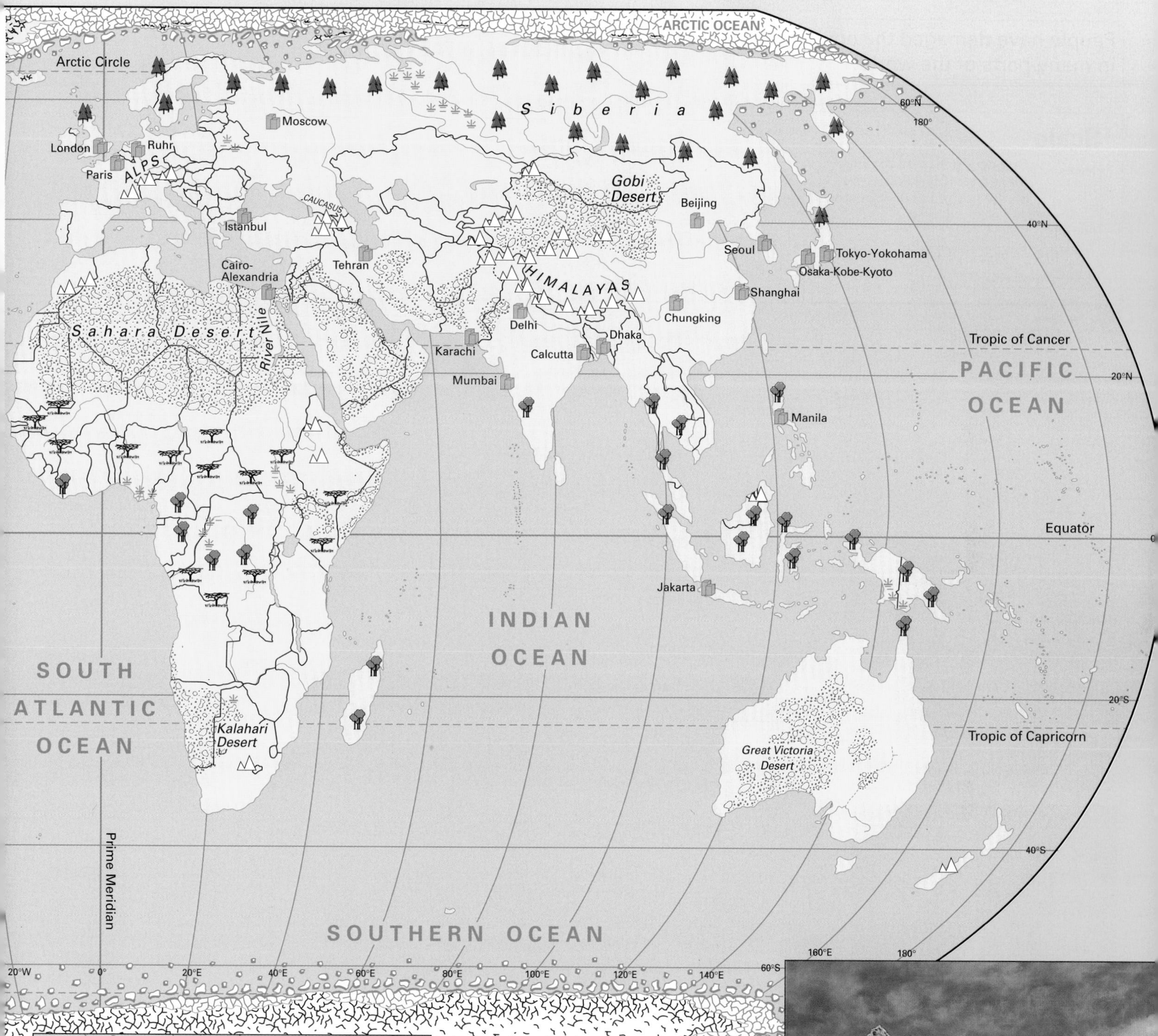
ARCTIC OCEAN
Arctic Circle
Siberia
Moscow
London
Ruhr
Paris
ALPS
CAUCASUS
Istanbul
Gobi Desert
Beijing
Seoul
Tokyo-Yokohama
Osaka-Kobe-Kyoto
Shanghai
Tehran
Cairo-Alexandria
HIMALAYAS
Sahara Desert
River Nile
Delhi
Chungking
Karachi
Dhaka
Calcutta
Mumbai
Tropic of Cancer
PACIFIC OCEAN
Manila
Equator
Jakarta
INDIAN OCEAN
SOUTH ATLANTIC OCEAN
Kalahari Desert
Great Victoria Desert
Tropic of Capricorn
Prime Meridian
SOUTHERN OCEAN
60°N
40°N
20°N
0°
20°S
40°S
60°S
180°
20°W
0°
20°E
40°E
60°E
80°E
100°E
120°E
140°E
160°E
180°

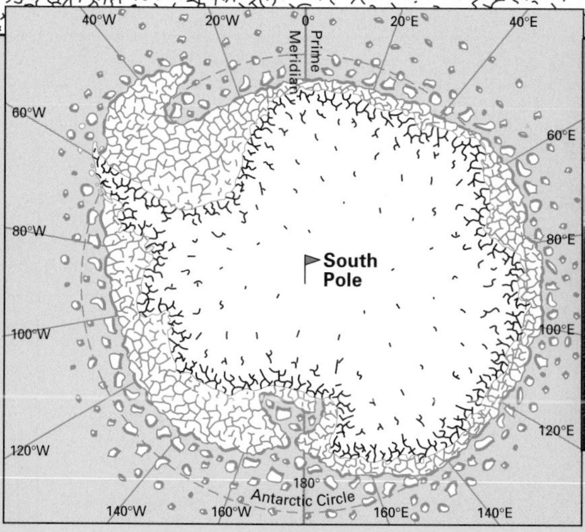
40°W
20°W
0°
20°E
40°E
Prime Meridian
60°W
60°E
80°W
80°E
South Pole
100°W
100°E
120°W
120°E
140°W
160°W
180°
Antarctic Circle
160°E
140°E

ice

high mountains

Eckert IV Projection

World Environmental problems

People have damaged the environment in many parts of the world.

Scale

One centimetre on the map measures 1050 kilometres on the ground at the Equator.

1050 km — one cm

0 | 1050 | 2100 | 3150 | 4200 km

acid rain
Jelenia Gora, Poland

nuclear accident
Chernobyl, Ukraine

forest loss
Trans-Amazonian Highway, Brazil

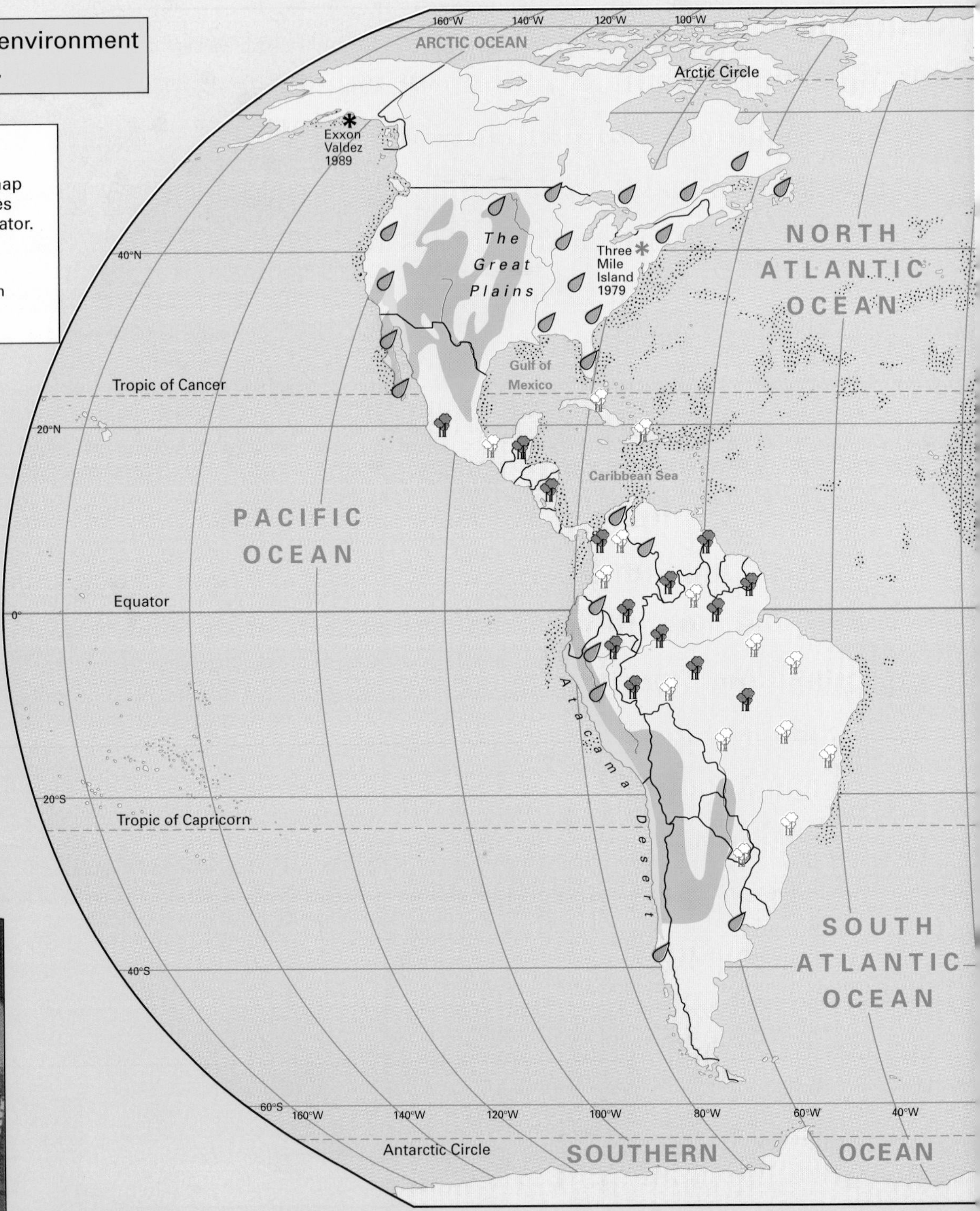

Key

- tropical rain forest
- worst areas of forest loss
- desert
- spreading edges of desert
- areas most affected by acid rain
- sea areas most likely to be affected by major oil pollution
- recent major oil spill
- recent major nuclear or chemical accident
- country boundary

Eckert IV Projection

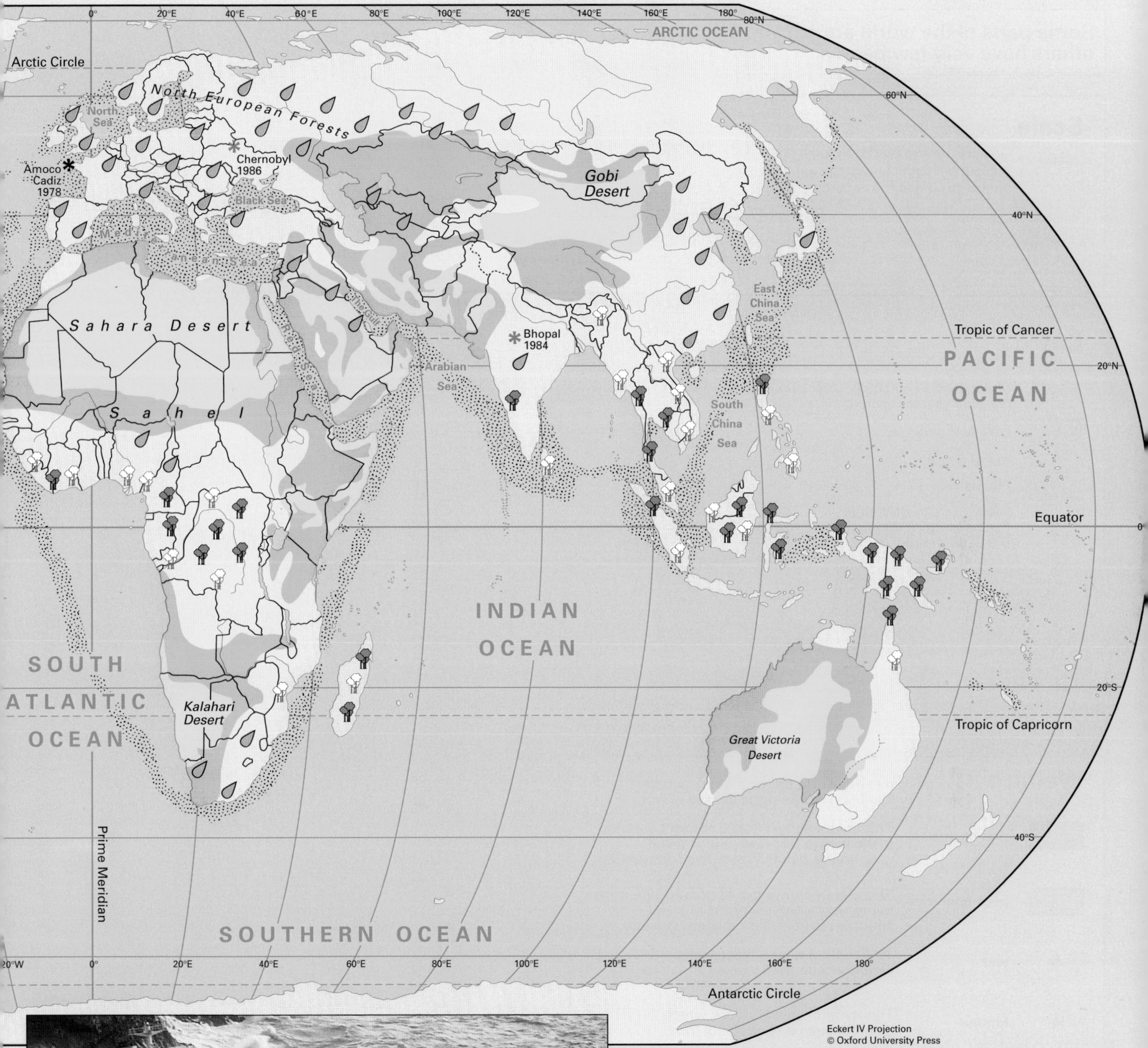

Eckert IV Projection

oil pollution
Shetland Islands, United Kingdom

spreading desert
The Sahel, Burkina

World People and cities

Some parts of the world are crowded, others have very few people.

Scale

1050 km

One centimetre on the map measures 1050 kilometres on the ground at the equator.

one cm

0 1050 2100 3150 4200 km

Key

- one million (1 000 000) people live near each dot
- very many people
- many people
- few people
- the world's largest cities. Each has more than 5 million people

Welfare

Some people in the world are rich. Many people are poor, or hungry, or suffering as a result of war.

	rich countries	This colour shows the 25 richest countries in the world. Not everyone in these countries is rich but most live comfortably.
	poor countries	This colour shows the 40 poorest countries in the world. Not everyone in these countries is poor but most are in need.
	war	This symbol shows places where there has recently been a war.
	famine	This symbol shows places where there has recently been a shortage of food.

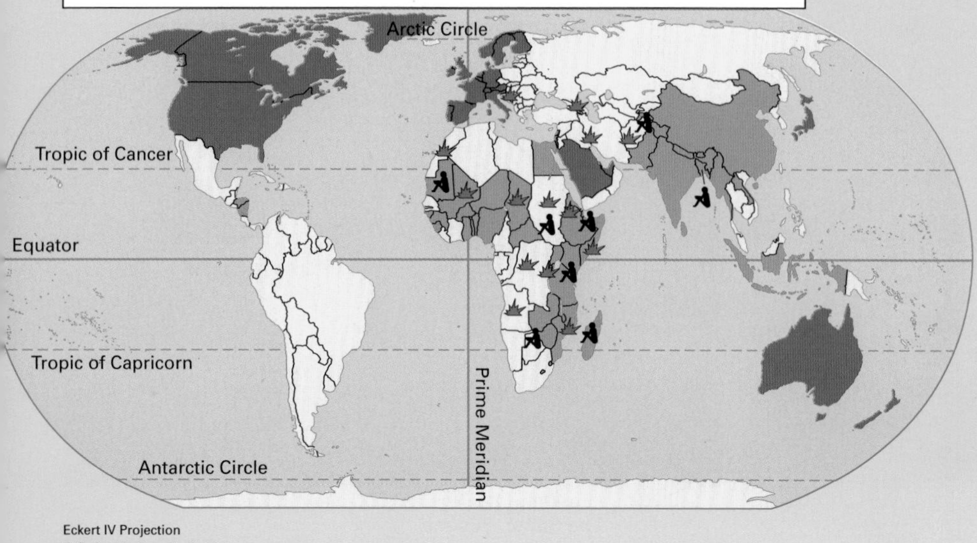

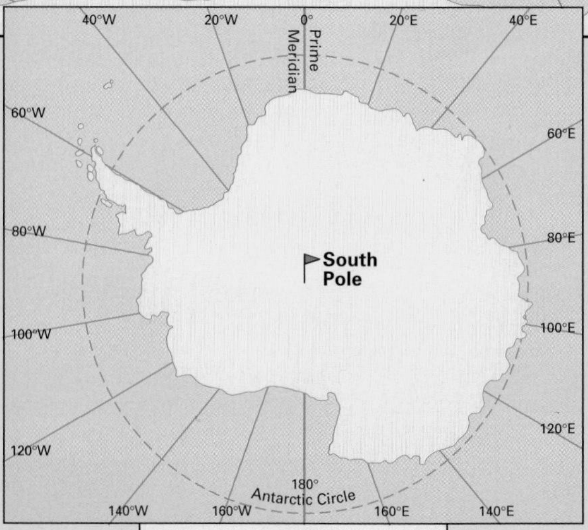

There are no permanent settlements in Antarctica.

Eckert IV Projection

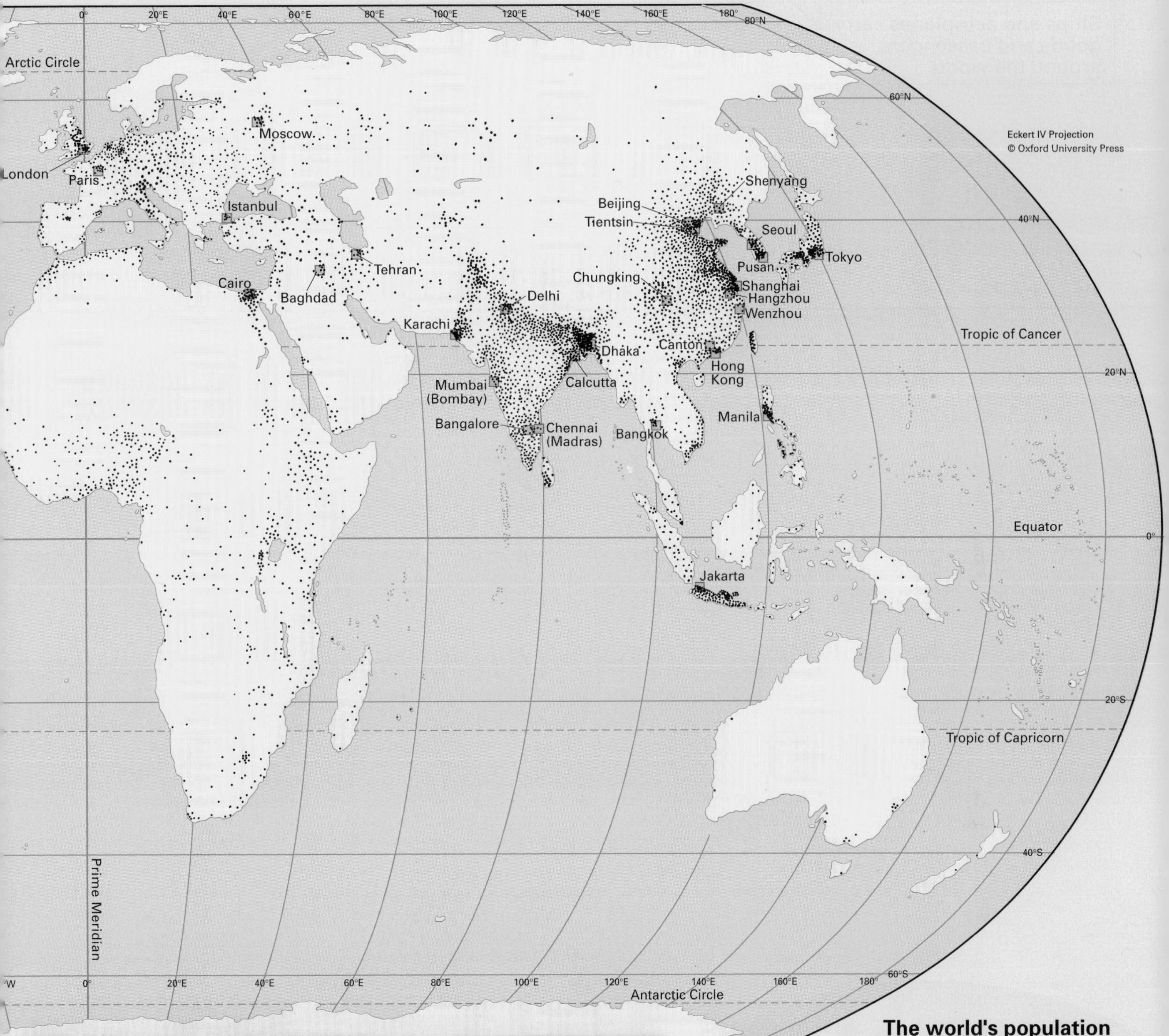
Eckert IV Projection
© Oxford University Press
Arctic Circle
Tropic of Cancer
Equator
Tropic of Capricorn
Antarctic Circle
Prime Meridian
0°
20°E
40°E
60°E
80°E
100°E
120°E
140°E
160°E
180°
80°N
60°N
40°N
20°N
0°
20°S
40°S
60°S
London
Paris
Moscow
Istanbul
Cairo
Baghdad
Tehran
Karachi
Delhi
Mumbai (Bombay)
Bangalore
Chennai (Madras)
Calcutta
Dhaka
Bangkok
Beijing
Tientsin
Shenyang
Seoul
Pusan
Tokyo
Chungking
Shanghai
Hangzhou
Wenzhou
Canton
Hong Kong
Manila
Jakarta

The world's population is growing very rapidly

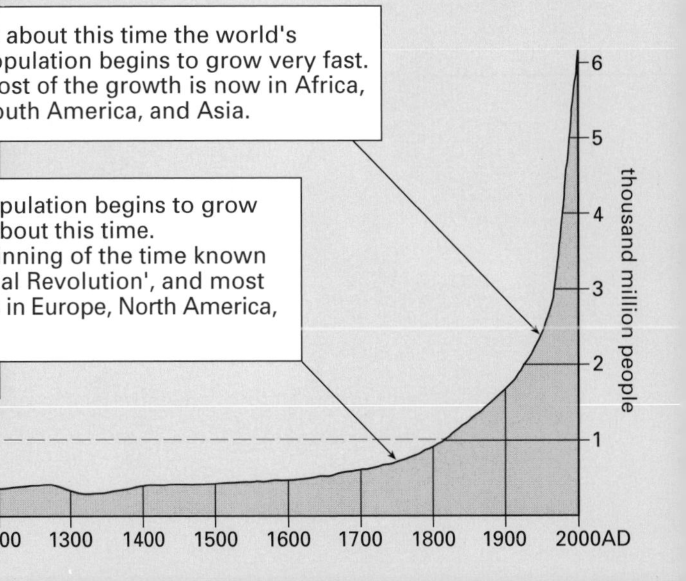
At about this time the world's population begins to grow very fast. Most of the growth is now in Africa, South America, and Asia.
The world's population begins to grow steadily from about this time. This is the beginning of the time known as the "Industrial Revolution', and most of the growth is in Europe, North America, and Oceania.
thousand million people
1
2
3
4
5
6
1AD
100
200
300
400
500
600
700
800
900
1000
1100
1200
1300
1400
1500
1600
1700
1800
1900
2000AD

Ships and aeroplanes carry goods and passengers around the world.

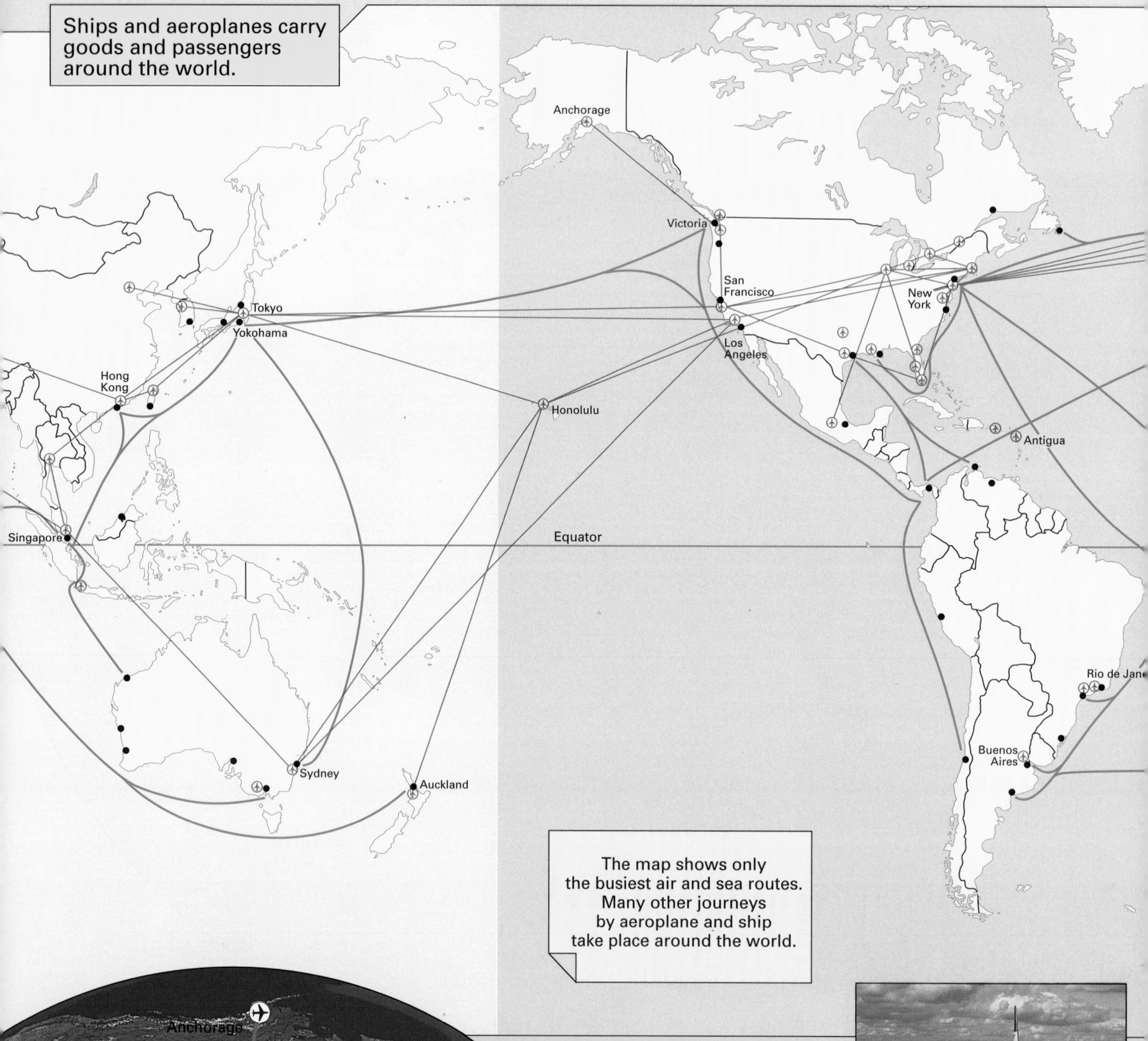

The map shows only the busiest air and sea routes. Many other journeys by aeroplane and ship take place around the world.

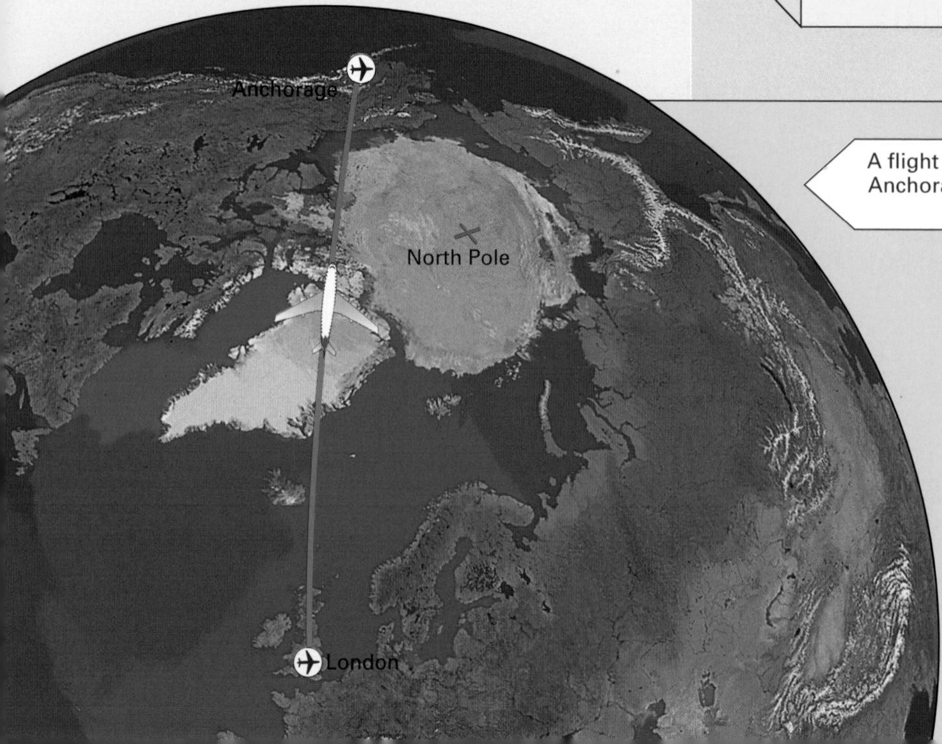

A flight from London to Anchorage passes near the North Pole.

This Boeing 747 takes 10.5 hours to fly from London Heathrow to Antigua.

Gall Projection

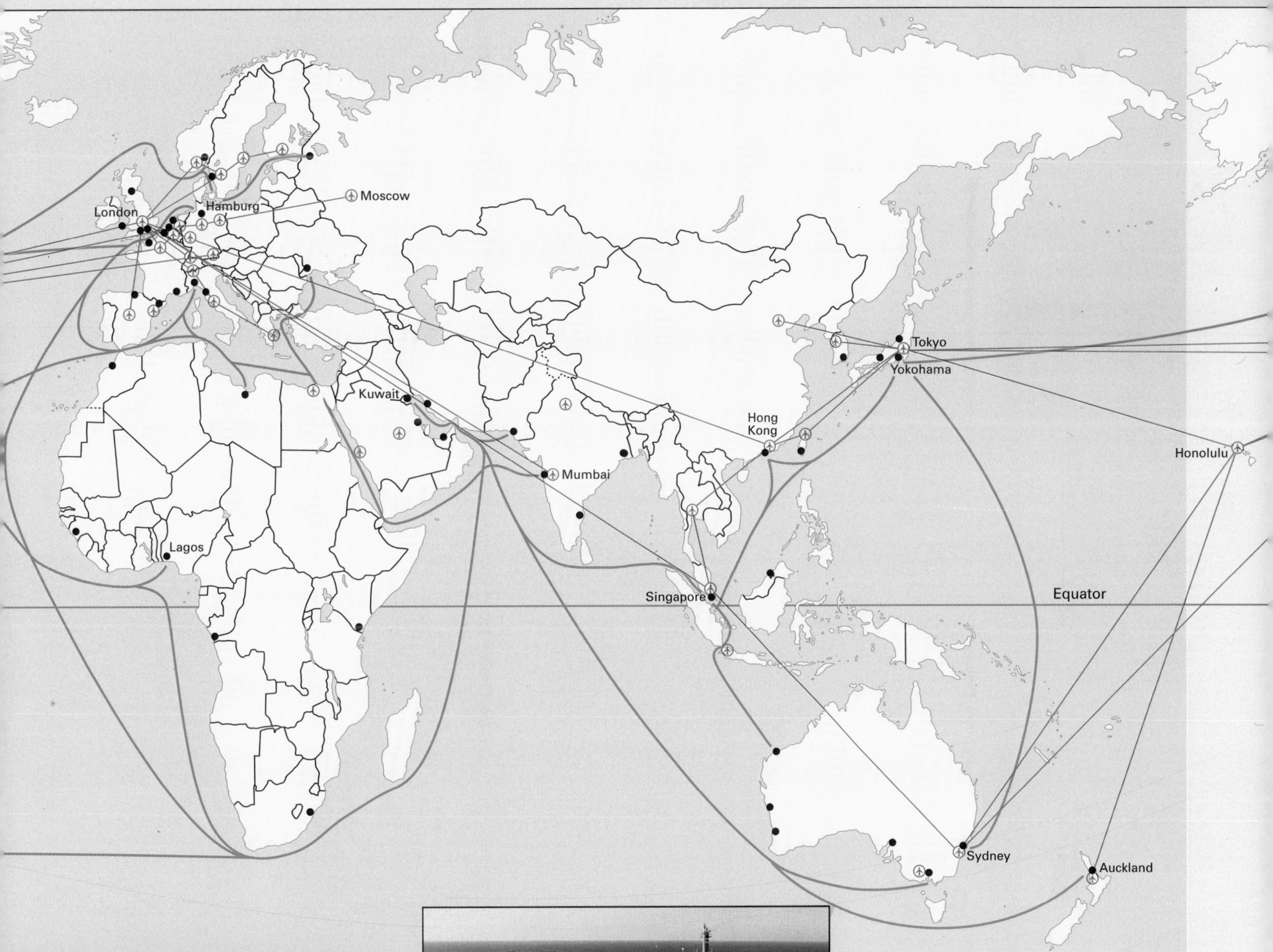

This oil tanker takes 18 days to sail from Kuwait to the United Kingdom.

his container ship takes 25 days to sail
rom Hamburg to Buenos Aires.

Scale

1200 km

one cm

One centimetre on the map measures 1200 kilometres on the ground at the Equator.

0 1200 2400 3600 4800 km

Key

international boundary

main shipping lanes

major port

main air routes

major airport

It is about 40 000 kilometres (25 000 miles) around the world.

Gall Projection

name of place — grid code

Telford 22 C1

page number

A

Aberaeron 24 C2
Aberchirder 19 G2
Aberdare 24 D1
Aberdeen 19 G2
Aberdeen City *unitary authority* 19 G2
Aberdeenshire *unitary authority* 19 F1/G2
Aberfeldy 19 F1
Abergavenny 24 D1
Abertillery 24 D1
Aberystwyth 24 C2
Abidjan 46 B4
Abingdon 25 F1
Aboyne 19 G2
Abu Dhabi 42 B4
Abuja 46 C4
Accra 46 B4
Adana 38 D1
Addis Ababa 46 D4
Adelaide 48 B2
Adriatic Sea 40 C2
Aegean Sea 40 D1
Afghanistan 42 C4
Ahmadabad 42 C4
Ailsa Craig *island* 20 D3
Airdrie 21 F3
Aire *river* 22 C2
Akmola 42 C5
Albania 38 C2/D2
Albany 48 A2
Aldabra Islands 47 E3
Aldeburgh 27 F3
Alderney *island* 29 E2
Aldershot 26 D2
Aleppo (Halab) 42 A4
Aleutian Islands 51 A3
Alexandria Egypt 46 D5
Alexandria UK 21 E3
Algeria 46 B5/C5
Algiers 46 C5
Alice Springs *town* 48 B2
Alloa 21 F4
Aln *river* 21 H3
Alnwick 21 H3
Alps *mountains* 40 C2
Altai Mountains 44 D5
Alton 29 G4
Alyth 19 F1
Amble 21 H3
Ambleside 21 G2
Amesbury 29 F4
Amman 42 A4
Amsterdam 38 C2
Amundsen Sea 54
Anatolian Plateau 40 D1/D2
Anchorage 50 B4
Andaman Islands 44 D3
Andaman Sea 44 D3
Andes *mountains* 53 C2/C4
Andorra 38 C2
Andover 29 F4
Angara River 44 D5
Angel Falls 53 C4
Anglesey *island* 24 C3
Angola 46 C3/D3
Angola Plateau 47 C3/D3
Angus *unitary authority* 19 G1
Ankara 38 D1
Annan 21 F2
Annan *river* 21 F3
Anshan 42 F5
Anstruther 21 G4
Antarctic Peninsula 54
Antigua and Barbuda 50 F1
Antofagasta 52 C2
Antrim 20 C2
Antrim *district* 20 C2
Antrim Mountains 20 C3/D2
Appalachian Mountains 51 E2/F3
Appennines *mountains* 40 C2
Appleby-in-Westmorland 21 G2
Arabian Peninsula 44 B4
Arabian Sea 44 C3
Aracaju 52 E3
Arafura Sea 49 B3
Aral Sea 44 C5
Arbroath 19 G1
Arctic Ocean 55
Ardbeg 20 C3
Ardminish 20 D3
Ardres 27 F1
Ards *district* 20 D2
Ards Peninsula 20 D2
Arequipa 52 C3
Argentina 52 C1/D2
Argyll and Bute *unitary authority* 18/19 C3/E1
Arica 52 C3
Arisaig 18 D1
Arkansas River 51 D2/E2
Arklow 24 A2
Armagh 20 C2
Armagh *district* 20 C2
Armenia 42 B5
Armentières 27 G1
Arnhem Land 49 B3
Arnold 23 D1
Arran *island* 20 D3
Aruba *island* 52 C4
Arun *river* 26 D2
Arundel 26 D1
Ashbourne 22 D2
Ashford 27 E2
Ashington 21 H3
Ashkhabad 42 B4
Asmara 46 D4
Asunción 52 D2
Atacama Desert 53 C2/C3
Athens 38 D1
Atlanta 50 E2
Atlantic Ocean 40 B2
Altas Mountains 47 B5/C5
Auchterarder 21 F4
Auchterrmuchty 19 F1
Auckland 48 D2
Auderville 29 F2
Australia 48 A2/C2
Australian Alps 49 C2
Austria 38 C2
Aviemore 19 F2
Avon Warwickshire *river* 25 F2
Avon Wiltshire *river* 29 E4
Axminster 29 E3
Ayers Rock *mountain* 49 B2
Aylesbury 26 D2
Ayr 21 E3
Ayr *river* 21 E3
Azerbaijan 42 B4/B5
Azores *islands* 47 A5

B

Baffin Bay 55
Baffin Island 51 F4
Baghdād 42 B4
Bahía Blanca 52 C2
Bahrain 42 B4
Baie de la Seine *bay* 29 G2
Bakewell 22 D2
Baku 42 B5
Bala 24 D2
Bala Lake (Llyn Tegid) 24 D2
Balearic Islands 40 C1
Bali *island* 44 E2
Ballantrae 20 D3
Ballater 19 F2
Ballybofey 20 B2
Ballycastle 20 C3
Ballymena 20 C2
Ballymena *district* 20 C2
Ballymoney 20 C3
Ballymoney *district* 20 C3
Ballyshannon 20 A2
Baltic Sea 40 C2
Baltimore 50 F2
Bamako 46 B4
Bamburgh 21 H3
Banbridge 20 C2
Banbridge *district* 20 C2
Banbury 25 F2
Banchory 19 G2
Bandar Seri Begawan 42 E3
Bandung 42 E2
Banff 19 G2
Bangalore 42 C3
Bangkok 42 E3
Bangladesh 42 C4
Bangor Northern Ireland 20 D2
Bangor Wales 24 C3
Bangui 46 C4
Banjul 46 B4
Banks Islands 49 D3
Bann *river* 20 C2
Barbados 50 F1
Barcelona Spain 38 C2
Barcelona Venezuela 52 C4
Barents Sea 55
Barfleur 29 F2
Barking 27 E2
Barmouth 24 C2
Barnard Castle 21 H2
Barnet 26 D2
Barnoldswick 22 C2
Barnsley 23 D2
Barnstaple 28 C4
Barra *island* 18 B1/B2
Barranquilla 52 C4
Barrow-in-Furness 21 F2
Barry 24 D1
Barton-upon-Humber 23 E2
Basildon 27 E2
Basingstoke 26 C2
Basra 42 B4
Bass Strait 49 C1/C2
Bath 29 E4
Bath and North East Somerset *unitary authority* 26 B2
Bathgate 21 F3
Bayeux 29 G2
Bay of Bengal 44 D3
Bay of Biscay 40 B2
Beachy Head 27 E1
Bearsden 21 E3
Beaufort Sea 55
Beauly *river* 19 E2
Beccles 27 F3
Bedford 26 D3
Bedfordshire *county* 26 D3
Bedworth 25 F2
Beijing (Peking) 42 E4
Beinn Dearg *mountain* 19 E2
Beira 46 D3
Beirut 42 A4
Belarus 38 D2
Belém 52 D3
Belfast 20 D2
Belfast *district* 20 C2/D2
Belfast Lough 20 D2
Belgium 38 C2
Belgrade 38 D2
Belize 50 E1
Bellingshausen Sea 54
Belmopan 50 E1
Belo Horizonte 52 D3
Ben Alder *mountain* 19 E1
Benbecula *island* 18 B2
Ben Cruachan *mountain* 19 D1
Benguela 46 C3
Ben Hope *mountain* 19 E3
Benin 46 C4
Ben Klibreck *mountain* 19 E3
Ben Lawers *mountain* 19 E1
Ben Lomond *mountain* 21 E4
Ben More *mountain* 18 C1
Ben More *mountain* 19 E1
Ben More Assynt *mountain* 19 E3
Ben Nevis *mountain* 19 E1
Ben Wyvis *mountain* 19 E2
Bergen 38 C3
Bering Sea 55
Bering Strait 55
Berlin 38 C2
Bermuda *island* 51 F2
Bern 38 C2
Berneray *island* 18 B2
Berwick-upon-Tweed 21 G3
Bethesda 24 C3
Béthune 27 G1
Beverley 23 E2
Bewdley 25 E2
Bexley 27 E2
Bhutan 42 D4
Bicester 25 F1
Bideford 28 C4
Bideford Bay 28 C4
Bigbury Bay 28 D3
Biggar 21 F3
Biggleswade 26 D3
Bilbao 38 B2
Birkenhead 22 B2
Birmingham 25 F2
Bishkek 42 C5
Bishop Auckland 21 H2
Bishop's Stortford 27 E2
Bissau 46 B4
Blackburn 22 C2
Blackburn and Darwen *unitary authority* 22 C2
Black Mountains 24 D1
Blackpool 22 B2
Blackpool *unitary authority* 22 B2
Black Sea 40/41 D2
Blackwater *river* 20 C2
Blackwater Reservoir 19 E1
Blaenau Ffestiniog 24 D2
Blaenau Gwent *unitary authority* 24 D1
Blairgowrie 19 F1
Blandford Forum 29 E3
Blantyre 46 D3
Blyth *river* 22 E4
Boa Vista 52 C4
Bodmin 28 C3
Bodmin Moor 28 C3
Bognor Regis 29 G3
Bogotá 52 C4
Bolivia 52 C3
Bolton 22 C2
Bombay *see* Mumbai
Bonar Bridge *town* 19 E2
Bo'ness 21 F4
Bonn 38 C2
Bootle 22 B2
Bordeaux 38 B2
Borneo *island* 44 E2/E3
Bornholm *island* 40 C2
Boscastle 28 C3
Bosnia-Herzegovina 38 C2
Boston UK 23 E1
Boston USA 50 F3
Botswana 46 D2
Boulogne-sur-Mer 27 F1
Bourke 48 C2
Bournemouth 29 F3
Bournemouth *unitary authority* 29 F3
Bovey Tracey 28 D3
Bracknell 26 D2
Bracknell Forest *unitary authority* 26 D2
Bradford 22 D2
Braemar 19 F2
Brahmaputra River 44 D4
Braintree 27 E2
Brampton 21 G2
Branderburgh 19 F2
Brásilia 52 D3
Bratislava 38 C2
Braunton 28 C4
Bray 24 A3
Brazil 52 C3/E3
Brazilian Highlands 53 D3
Brazil Plateau 53 D2/D3
Brazzaville 46 C3
Brechin 19 G1
Brecon 24 D1
Brecon Beacons *mountains* 24 D1
Brent 26 D2
Brentwood 27 E2
Bressay 17 D3
Bridgend 24 D1
Bridgend *unitary authority* 24 D1
Bridgnorth 25 E2
Bridgwater 29 D3
Bridgewater Bay 29 D4
Bridlington 23 D3
Bridport 29 E3
Brigg 23 E2
Brighouse 22 D2
Brighton 26 D1
Brighton and Hove *unitary authority* 26 D1
Brisbane 48 C2
Bristol 29 E4
Bristol *unitary authority* 26 B2
Bristol Channel 24 C1/D1
Broad Bay 18 C3
Broadford 18 D2
Broad Law 21 F3
Broadway 25 F2
Brodick 20 D3
Broken Hill *town* 48 C2
Bromley 27 E2
Bromsgrove 25 E2
Bromyard 25 E2
Broome 48 B3
Brora 19 F3
Brough 21 G2
Brough Head 17 B2
Brown Clee Hill 25 E2
Brown Willy *summit* 28 C3
Bruay-en-Artois 27 G1
Brunei Darussalam 42 E3
Brussels 38 C2
Buchan Ness 19 H2
Bucharest 38 D2
Buckfastleigh 28 D3
Buckhaven 21 F4
Buckie 19 G2
Buckingham 26 D2
Buckinghamshire *county* 26 D2
Budapest 38 C2
Bude 28 C3
Bude Bay 28 C3
Buenaventura 52 C4
Buenos Aires 52 D2
Buffalo 50 F3
Builth Wells 24 D2
Bujumbura 46 D3
Bulgaria 38 D2
Buncrana 20 B3
Bure *river* 27 F3
Burghead *town* 19 F2
Burkina 46 B4
Burnley 22 C2
Burry Port 24 C1
Bursa 38 D2
Burton upon Trent 22 D1
Bury 22 C2
Bury St. Edmunds 27 E3
Bush *river* 20 C3
Bushehr 42 B4
Bute *island* 20 D3
Butt of Lewis *cape* 18 C3
Buxton 22 D2

C

Cader Idris *mountain* 24 D2
Caen 29 G2
Caernarfon 24 C3
Caernarfon Bay 24 C3
Caerphilly 24 D1
Caerphilly *unitary authority* 24 D1
Cairn Gorm *mountain* 19 F2
Cairngorms *mountains* 19 F2
Cairns 48 C3
Calais 27 F1
Calgary 50 D3
Cali 52 C4
Callander 21 E4
Calligarry 18 D2
Calne 29 E4
Cam *river* 27 E3
Camberley 26 D2
Cambodia 42 E3
Camborne 28 B3
Cambrian Mountains 24 D2
Cambridge 27 E3
Cambridgeshire *county* 26/27 D3/E3
Camel *river* 28 C3
Cameroon 46 C4
Campbeltown 20 D3
Campsie Fells *hills* 21 E4
Canada 50 C3/F4
Canary Islands 47 B5
Canberra 48 C2
Canisp *mountain* 19 D3
Canna *island* 18 C2
Cannock 22 C1
Canterbury 27 F2
Cap de la Hague *cape* 29 F2
Cape Horn 53 C1
Cape of Good Hope 47 C2
Cape Town 46 C2
Cape Verde Islands 47 A4
Cape Wrath 19 D3
Cape York Peninsula 49 C3
Cap Gris-Nez *cape* 27 F1
Caracas 52 C4
Cardiff 24 D1
Cardiff *unitary authority* 24 D1
Cardigan 24 C2
Cardigan Bay 24 C2
Carentan 29 F2
Caribbean Sea 51 F1
Carlingford Lough *bay* 20 C2
Carlisle 21 G2
Carmarthen 24 C1
Carmarthen Bay 24 C1
Carmarthenshire *unitary authority* 24 C1/D1
Carmel Head 24 C3
Carn Eige *mountain* 19 D2
Carnforth 22 D3
Carnoustie 19 G1
Caroline Islands 49 C4
Carpathians *mountains* 40 C2/D2
Carrickfergus 20 D2
Carrickfergus *district* 20 D2
Carrickmacross 20 C1
Carrick-on-Shannon 20 A1
Cartagena 52 C4
Carteret 29 F2
Casablanca 46 B5
Caspian Sea 41 E1/E2
Cassel 27 G1
Castlebay 18 B1
Castleblaney 20 C2
Castle Douglas 21 F2
Castleford 23 D2
Castlereagh *county* 20 D2
Castletown 21 E2
Caucasus *mountains* 41 E2
Cavan 20 B1
Cavan *county* 20 B1/B2
Cayenne 52 D4
Cemaes Head 24 C2
Central African Republic 46 C4/D4
Central Siberian Plateau 44 E6/F6
Ceredigion *unitary authority* 24 C2/D2
Chad 46 C4/D4
Changchun 42 F5
Channel Islands 29 E2
Chard 29 E3
Charlestown of Aberlour 19 F2
Charlotte 50 E2
Chatham 27 E2
Cheadle 22 C2
Chelmsford 27 E2
Cheltenham 25 E1
Chelyabinsk 42 C5
Chengdu 42 E4
Chennai 42 D3
Chepstow 25 E1
Cherbourg 38 B2
Cherwell *river* 25 F1
Cheshire *county* 22 C2
Cheshunt 26 D2
Chester 22 C2
Chesterfield 23 D2
Chester-le-Street 21 H2
Cheviot Hills 21 G3
Chicago 50 E3
Chichester 29 G3

Chile 52 C1/C2
Chiltern Hills 26 C2/D2
Chimborazo *mountain* 53 C3
China 42 E4/F4
Chippenham 29 E4
Chipping Norton 25 F1
Chittagong 42 D4
Chongqing 42 E4
Chorley 22 C2
Chişnău 38 D2
Christchurch New Zealand 48 D1
Christchurch UK 29 F3
Cincinnati 50 E2
Cirencester 25 F1
Citlaltépetl *mountain* 51 E1
City of Edinburgh *unitary authority* 21 F3
City of Kingston upon Hull *unitary authority* 23 E2
Ciudad Bolívar 52 C4
Ciudad Guayana 52 C4
Clachan 20 D3
Clackmannanshire *unitary authority* 21 F4
Clacton on Sea 27 F2
Claonaig 20 D3
Cleethorpes 23 E2
Clevedon 29 E4
Cleveland 50 E3
Cleveland Hills 23 D3
Clisham *mountain* 18 C2
Clitheroe 22 C2
Clones 20 B2
Clwyd *river* 24 D3
Clyde *river* 21 F3
Clydebank 21 E3
Coalisland 20 C2
Coalville 23 D1
Coatbridge 21 E3
Cockermouth 21 F2
Colchester 27 E2
Coldstream 21 G3
Coleraine 20 C3
Coleraine *district* 20 C3
Coll *island* 18 C1
Colne 22 C2
Colne *river* 27 E2
Colombia 52 C4
Colombo 42 C3
Colonsay *island* 20 C4
Colorado River 51 D2
Columbus 50 E2
Colwyn Bay *town* 24 D3
Communism Peak 44 C4
Comodoro Rivadavia 52 C1
Comoro Archipelago *islands* 47 E3
Comoros 46 E3
Conakry 46 B4
Concepción 52 C2
Congo 46 C3/C4
Congo, Democratic Republic 46 C3/D3
Coniston Water *lake* 21 F2
Consett 21 H2
Conwy 24 D3
Conwy *river* 24 D3
Conwy *unitary authority* 24 D3
Cookstown 20 C2
Cookstown *district* 20 C2
Cook Strait 49 D1/D2
Copenhagen 38 C2
Coquet *river* 21 G3
Coral Sea 49 C3
Córdoba 52 C2
Cork 38 B2
Cornwall *county* 28 B3/C3
Corsewall Point 20 D3
Corsica 40 C2
Costa Rica 50 E1
Côte d'Ivoire 46 B4
Cotopaxi *mountain* 53 C3
Cotswold Hills 25 E1
Coupar Angus 19 F1
Coutainville 29 F2
Coutances 29 F2
Coventry 25 F2
Cowes 29 F3
Craigavon 20 C2
Craigavon *district* 20 C2
Craighouse 20 D3
Craignure 18 D1
Crail 21 G4
Cramlington 21 H3
Crawley 26 D2
Crediton 28 D3
Cree *river* 21 E3
Creeslough 20 B3
Crete 40 D1
Crewe 22 C2
Crewkerne 29 E3
Crianlarich 19 E1
Crieff 19 F1
Croatia 38 C2
Cromarty 19 E2
Cromarty Firth *estuary* 19 E2
Cromer 27 F3
Cross Fell *summit* 21 G2
Crossmaglen 20 C2
Croydon 26 D2
Crumlin 20 C2
Cuba 50 E2
Cuiabá 52 D3
Cuillin Hills 18 C2
Cullen 19 G2
Cullompton 28 D3
Cumbernauld 21 F3
Cumbria *county* 21 F2/G2
Cumbrian Mountains 21 F2/G2
Cumnock 21 E3
Cunnamulla 48 C2
Cupar 19 F1
Curitiba 52 D2
Cuzco 52 C3
Cwmbran 24 D1
Cyprus 38 D1
Czech Republic 38 C2

D

Daer Reservoir 21 F3
Dakar 46 B4
Dalbeattie 21 F2
Dalian 42 F4
Dallas 50 E2
Dalmally 19 E1
Dalton-in-Furness 21 F2
Damascus 42 A4
Dandong 42 F5
Dar es Salaam 46 D3
Darling River 49 C2
Darlington 21 H2
Darlington *unitary authority* 22 D3
Dart *river* 28 D3
Dartford 27 E2
Dartmoor 28 D3
Dartmouth 28 D3
Darvel 21 E3
Darwin 48 B3
Daventry 25 F2
Davis Strait 51 G4
Dawlish 28 D3
Dead Sea 44 A4
Deal 27 F2
Death Valley 51 D2
Deccan *plateau* 44 C3
Dee Aberdeenshire *river* 19 G2
Dee Dumfries and Galloway *river* 21 E2
Delhi 42 C4
Denbigh 24 D3
Denbighshire *unitary authority* 24 D3
Denmark 38 C2
Denver 50 D2
De Panne 27 G2
Derby 23 D1
Derby City *unitary authority* 22/23 D1
Derbyshire *county* 22 D2
Derwent Cumbria *river* 21 F2
Derwent Derbyshire *river* 22 D2
Derwent Durham/Northumberland *river* 21 G2
Derwent North Yorkshire *river* 23 E2
Derwent Water 21 F2
Detroit 50 E3
Deveron *river* 19 G2
Devon *county* 28 C3/D3
Dewsbury 22 D2
Dhaka 42 D4
Didcot 25 F1
Dingwall 19 E2
Diss 27 F3
Djibouti 46 E4
Djibouti 46 E4
Dnepropetrovsk 38 D2
Dodoma 46 D3
Doha 42 B4
Dolgellau 24 D2
Dominica 50 F1
Dominican Republic 50 F1
Don *river* 19 G2
Donaghadee 20 D2
Doncaster 23 D2
Donegal 20 A2
Donegal *county* 20 A2/B2
Donetsk 39 D2
Doon *river* 21 E3
Dorchester 29 E3
Dornoch 19 E2
Dornoch Firth *estuary* 19 E2
Dorset *county* 29 E3
Douala 46 C4
Douglas 21 E2
Dove *river* 22 D2
Dover 27 F2
Dovey *river* 24 D2
Down *district* 20 D2
Downham Market 27 E3
Downpatrick 20 D2
Drakensberg *mountains* 47 D2
Droitwich 25 E2
Dromore 20 C2
Drummore 20 E2
Drumnadrochit 19 E2
Dublin 38 B2
Dudley 25 E2
Dufftown 19 F2
Dumbarton 21 E3
Dumfries 21 F3
Dumfries and Galloway *unitary authority* 21 E3/F3
Dunbar 21 G4
Dunblane 21 F4
Duncansby Head 19 F3
Dundalk 20 C2
Dundee 19 G1
Dundee City *unitary authority* 19 F1/G1
Dunedin 48 D1
Dunfermline 21 F4
Dungannon 20 C2
Dungannon *district* 20 B2/C2
Dungeness *cape* 27 E1
Dungiven 20 C2
Dunkerque 27 G2
Dunkery Beacon *summit* 28 D4
Dún Laoghaire 24 A3
Dunnett Head 19 F3
Dunoon 20 E3
Duns 21 G3
Dunvegan 18 C2
Durban 46 D2
Durham 21 H2
Durham *county* 21 G2/H2
Dursley 25 E1
Dushanbe 42 C4
Dyce 19 G2

E

Ealing 26 D2
Earn *river* 19 F1
East Ayrshire *unitary authority* 21 E3
Eastbourne 27 E1
East China Sea 44 F4
East Dereham 27 E3
East Dunbartonshire *unitary authority* 21 E3
East Kilbride 21 E3
Eastleigh 29 F3
East London 46 D2
East Lothian *unitary authority* 21 G3
East Renfrewshire *unitary authority* 21 E3
East Riding of Yorkshire *unitary authority* 23 E2/E3
East Sussex *county* 27 E1
Ebbw Vale 24 D1
Ecuador 52 C3/C4
Eday *island* 17 C2
Eddrachillis Bay 18 D3
Eden Cumbria *river* 21 G2
Eden Kent *river* 27 E2
Edinburgh 21 F3
Edmonton 50 D3
Egypt 46 D5
Eigg *island* 18 C1
El Aaiún 46 B5
Elgin 19 F2
El Gîza 46 D5
Elgol 18 C2
Ellen *river* 21 F2
Ellesmere Port 22 C2
Ellon 19 G2
El Paso 50 D2
El Salvador 50 E1
Elsworth Land 54
Ely 27 E3
Enard Bay 18 D3
Enfield 26 D2
England 12
English Channel 40 B2
Enniskillen 20 B2
Epsom 26 D2
Equatorial Guinea 46 C4
Eriskay *island* 18 B2
Eritrea 46 D4/E4
Erne *river* 20 B2
Errigal Mountain 20 A3
Esfahan 42 B4
Esha Ness 17 D3
Esk Cumbria/Dumfries and Galloway *river* 21 F3
Esk North Yorkshire *river* 23 E3
Esperance 48 B2
Espiritu Santo *island* 49 D3
Essex *county* 27 E2
Estonia 38 D2
Ethiopia 46 D4/E4
Ethiopian Highlands 47 D4/E4
Evesham 25 F2
Exe *river* 28 D4
Exeter 28 D3
Exmoor 28 D4
Exmouth 28 D3
Eyemouth 21 G3
Eye Peninsula 18 C3

F

Faeroe Islands 40 B3
Fair Head *cape* 20 C3
Fair Isle 17 D2
Fakenham 27 E3
Fal *river* 28 C3
Falkirk 21 F3
Falkirk *unitary authority* 21 F3/F4
Falkland Islands 52 C1/D1
Falmouth 28 B3
Fareham 29 F3
Faringdon 25 F1
Farnborough 26 D2
Farnham 26 D2
Fawley 29 F3
Felixstowe 27 F2
Fermanagh *district* 20 B2
Fetlar *island* 17 E3
Fianarantsoa 46 E2
Fife *unitary authority* 21 F4/G4
Fiji 48 D3
Fiji Islands 49 D3
Filchner Ice Shelf 54
Finland 38 D3
Finn *river* 20 B2
Fionnphort 18 C1
Firth of Clyde *estuary* 20 D3/E3
Firth of Forth *estuary* 21 F4/G4
Firth of Lorn *estuary* 18 D1
Firth of Tay *estuary* 19 F1
Fishguard 24 C1
Flamborough Head *cape* 23 D3
Fleetwood 22 B2
Flinders Range *mountains* 49 B2
Flint 24 D3
Flintshire *unitary authority* 24 D3
Fochabers 19 F2
Folkestone 27 F2
Fora Ness *point* 17 D3
Forest of Bowland *hills* 22 D3/D4
Formby 22 B2
Forres 19 F2
Fortaleza 52 E3
Fort Augustus 19 E2
Forth *river* 21 E4
Fort William 19 D1
Foula *island* 17 C3
Fowey 28 C3
Fowey *river* 28 C3
Foyle *river* 20 B2
France 38 B2/C2
Fraserburgh 19 G2
Fraser River 51 C3
Freetown 46 B4
French Guiana 52 D4
Friesian Islands 40 C2
Frome 29 E4
Frome *river* 29 E3
Furnace 20 D4
Fushun 42 F5
FYROM (Former Yugoslav Republic of Macedonia) 38 D2

G

Gabon 46 C3/C4
Gaborone 46 D2
Gainsborough 23 E2
Gairloch *town* 18 D2
Galapagos Islands 53 B3
Galashiels 21 G3
Galdhøpiggen *mountain* 40 C3
Gatehouse of Fleet 21 E2
Gateshead 21 H2
Gdańsk 38 C2
Georgetown 52 D4
Georgia 39 E1
Geraldton 48 A2
Germany 38 C2
Ghana 46 B4
Gigha *island* 20 D3
Gilbert Islands 49 D3
Gillingham 27 E2
Girvan 20 E3
Gisborne 48 D2
Glasgow 21 E3
Glasgow City *unitary authority* 21 E3
Glastonbury 29 E4
Glenluce 21 E2
Glenrothes 21 F4
Gloucester 25 E1
Gloucestershire *county* 25 E1
Goat Fell *mountain* 20 D3
Gobi Desert 44 E5
Goiânia 52 D3
Goole 23 E2
Göteborg 38 C2
Gotland *island* 40 C2
Gower *peninsula* 24 C1
Grampian Mountains 19 E1/F1
Gran Chaco *geog. region* 53 C2/C3
Grangemouth 21 F4
Grantham 23 E1
Grantown-on-Spey 19 F2
Gravesend 27 E2
Great Australian Bight *bay* 49 B2
Great Barrier Reef 49 C3
Great Bear Lake 51 C4/D4
Great Britain 40 B2
Great Dividing Range *mountains* 49 C2/D2
Great Driffield 23 E3
Greater Antilles *islands* 51 F1
Greater London *county* 26 D2
Greater Manchester *county* 22 C2
Great Malvern 25 E2
Great Ouse *river* 27 E3
Great Plains 51 D3
Great Sandy Desert 49 B2
Great Slave Lake 51 D4
Great Stour *river* 27 F2
Great Torrington 28 C3
Great Victoria Desert 49 B2
Great Whernside *summit* 21 H2
Great Yarmouth 27 F3
Greece 38 D1/D2
Greenland 55
Greenock 21 E3
Greenwich 26 D2
Grenada 50 F1
Greta *river* 21 G2
Greymouth 48 D1
Greystones 24 A3
Grimsby 23 E2
Guadalajara 50 D2
Guangzhou 42 E4
Guatemala 50 E1
Guatemala 50 E1
Guayaquil 52 B2
Guernsey *island* 29 E2
Guiana Highlands 53 C4/D4
Guildford 26 D2
Guinea 46 B4
Guinea-Bissau 46 B4
Guisborough 23 D3
Gulf of Alaska 51 B3
Gulf of Bothnia 40 C3/D3
Gulf of California 51 D2
Gulf of Carpentaria 49 B3/C3
Gulf of Mexico 51 E2
Gulf of Thailand 44 E3
Gur'yev 42 B5
Guyana 52 D4
Gwynedd *unitary authority* 24 C2/D2

H

Haiti 50 F1
Halesowen 25 E2
Halifax Canada 50 F3
Halifax UK 22 D2
Halkirk 19 F3
Halton *unitary authority* 22 C2
Haltwhistle 21 G2
Hamburg 38 C2
Hamersley Range *mountains* 49 A2/B2
Hamilton Canada 50 F3
Hamilton New Zealand 48 D2
Hamilton UK 21 E3
Hampshire *county* 29 F4
Hampshire Downs *hills* 29 F4
Hangzhou 42 F4
Hanoi 42 E4
Harare 46 D3
Harbin 42 F5
Harlech 24 C2
Haroldswick 17 E3
Harris *island* 18 C2
Harrogate 22 D2
Harrow 26 D2
Hartford 50 F3
Hartland Point 28 C4
Hartlepool 23 D3
Hartlepool *unitary authority* 23 D3
Harwich 27 F2
Haslemere 26 D2
Hastings 27 E1
Hatherleigh 28 C3
Havana 50 E2
Havant 29 G3
Haverfordwest 24 C1
Haverhill 27 E3
Havering 27 E2
Hawaiian Islands 51 B2
Hawick 21 G3
Hay-on-Wye 24 D2
Hay River *town* 50 D4
Haywards Heath 26 D2
Hebrides *islands* 18 B1/C3
Helensburgh 21 E4
Helmsdale 19 F3
Helmsdale *river* 19 F3
Helsinki 38 D3
Helston 28 B3
Helvellyn *mountain* 21 F2
Hemel Hempstead 26 D2
Hemsworth 23 D2
Henley-on-Thames 26 D2
Hereford 25 E2
Herefordshire *unitary authority* 25 E2
Herma Ness 17 E3
Hertfordshire *county* 26 D2
Hexham 21 G2
Heysham 22 D3
Highland *unitary authority* 18/19 D2/E2
High Wycombe 26 D2
Hillingdon 26 D2
Himalayas *mountains* 44 D4
Hinckley 25 F2
Hindu Kush *mountains* 44 C4
Hitchin 26 D2
Hobart 48 C1
Ho Chi Minh 42 E3
Hokkaido *island* 44 G5

Holderness **23** E2
Holsworthy **28** C3
Holyhead **24** C3
Holy Island **24** C3
Holy Island (Lindisfarne) **21** H3
Honduras **50** E1
Hong Kong **42** E4
Honiara **48** D3
Honiton **29** D3
Honshu *island* **44** F4/G4
Horncastle **23** E2
Hornsea **23** E2
Horsham **26** D2
Hounslow **26** D2
Houston **50** E2
Hove **26** D1
Howth **24** A3
Hoy *island* **17** B1
Huddersfield **22** D2
Hudson Bay **51** E3
Hugh Town **28** A2
Hull *river* **23** E2
Humber *river* **23** E2
Hungary **38** C2/D2
Hunstanton **27** E3
Huntingdon **26** D3
Huntly **19** G2
Hwang-Ho River **44** E4
Hyderabad **42** C3

I

Ibadan **46** C4
Ibiza **40** C1
Iceland **38**
Ieper **27** G1
Ilchester **29** E3
Ilfracombe **28** C4
Ilkeston **23** D1
Ilkley **22** D2
Ilminster **29** E3
Immingham **23** E2
India **42** C4/D3
Indianapolis **50** E2
Indian Ocean **44** C2/D2
Indonesia **42** E2
Ingleborough *summit* **21** G2
Inishowen Peninsula **20** B3
Inner Hebrides *islands* **18** C1/C2
Innerleithen **21** F3
Inner Sound **18** D2
Inuvik **50** C4
Inverary **20** D4
Inverbervie **19** G1
Invercargill **48** D1
Inverclyde *unitary authority* **21** E3
Invergarry **19** E2
Invergordon **19** E2
Inverkeithing **21** F4
Invermoriston **19** E2
Inverness **19** E2
Inverurie **19** G2
Iona *island* **18** C1
Ionian Sea **40** C1
Ipswich **27** F3
Iquitos **52** C3
Iran **42** B4
Iraq **42** B4
Ireland *island* **40** B2
Irish Sea **24** B2
Irrawaddy River **44** D4
Irthing *river* **21** G2
Irvine **21** E3
Isigny-sur-Mer **29** F2
Isla *river* **19** F1
Islamabad **42** C4
Island Magee **20** D2
Islay *island* **20** C3
Isle of Anglesey *unitary authority* **24** C3
Isle of Man **12**
Isle of Wight *unitary authority* **29** F3
Isles of Scilly **28** A2
Israel **42** A4
Istanbul **38** D2
Italy **38** C1/C2
Itchen *river* **29** F4
Izmir **38** D1

J

Jacksonville **50** E2
Jakarta **42** E2
Jamaica **50** F1
Japan **42** F4/G5
Java *island* **44** E2
Java Sea **44** E2
Jaya Peak *mountain* **44** F2
Jedburgh **21** G3
Jersey *island* **29** E2
Jerusalem **42** A4
Jiddah **42** A4
Jilin **42** F5
Jinan **42** E4
Jinzhou **42** F5
João Pessoa **52** E3
Johannesburg **46** D2
John o'Groats **19** F3
Johnstone **21** E3
Jordan **42** A4
Juan Fernández Islands **53** C2
Jura *island* **20** D3/D4

K

Kabul **42** C4
Kalahari Desert **47** C2/D2
Kalgoorlie **48** B2
Kaliningrad **38** D2
Kamchatka Peninsula **45** G5
Kampala **46** D4
Kananga **46** D3
Kano **46** C4
Kanpur **42** D4
Kansas City **50** E2
Kao-hsiung **42** F4
Karachi **42** C4
Kathmandu **42** D4
Kazakhstan **42** C5
Kazan **42** B5
Keady **20** C2
Keighley **22** D2
Keith **19** G2
Kelso **21** G3
Kendal **21** G2
Kenilworth **25** F2
Kent *county* **27** E2
Kenya **46** D3/D4
Kerrera *island* **20** D1
Keswick **21** F2
Kettering **26** D3
Keynsham **29** E4
Kharkov **38** D2
Khartoum **46** D4
Kidderminster **25** E2
Kidsgrove **22** C2
Kidwelly **24** C1
Kielder Water *reservoir* **21** G3
Kiev **38** D2
Kigali **46** D3
Kilbrannan Sound **20** D3
Kilkeel **20** C2
Kilmacrenan **20** B3
Kilmaluag **18** C2
Kilmarnock **21** E3
Kilmory **20** D3
Kinbrace **19** F3
Kingsbridge **28** D3
King's Lynn **27** E3
Kingston **50** F1
Kingston upon Hull **23** E2
Kingston-upon-Thames **26** D2
Kingswood **29** E4
Kington **24** D2
Kingussie **19** E2
Kinloch **18** C2
Kinross **21** F4
Kinshasa **46** C3
Kintyre **20** D3
Kirgyzstan **42** C5
Kiribati **48** D3
Kirkbean **21** F2
Kirkby **22** C2
Kirkby Stephen **21** G2
Kirkcaldy **21** F4
Kirkcudbright **21** E2
Kirkintilloch **21** E3
Kirk Michael **21** E2
Kirkwall **17** C1
Kirriemuir **19** F1
Kita Kyushu **42** F4
Knaresborough **23** D3
Knighton **24** D2
Kola Peninsula **40/41** D3
Konya **38** D1
Korean Peninsula **44** F4
Kuala Lumpur **42** E3
Kunlun Shan *mountains* **44** C4/D4
Kuril Islands **45** G5
Kuwait **42** B4
Kuwait City **42** B4
Kyle of Lochalsh **18** D2
Kyushu *island* **44** F4

L

Labrador **51** F3/G3
Lagos **46** C4
Lahore **42** C4
Lairg **19** E3
Lake Asal **47** E4
Lake Balkhash **44** C5
Lake Baykal **44** E5
Lake Chad **47** C4
Lake Erie **51** E3
Lake Eyre **49** B2
Lake Huron **51** E3
Lake Ladoga **40** D3
Lake Maracaibo **53** C4
Lake Michigan **51** E3
Lake Nasser **47** D5
Lake Nyasa (Lake Malawi) **47** D3
Lake Onega **40** D3
Lake Ontario **51** F3
Lake Peipus **40** D2
Lake Superior **51** E3
Lake Tanganyika **47** D3
Lake Taupo **49** D2
Lake Titicaca **53** C3
Lake Turkana **47** D4
Lake Van **41** E1
Lake Vänern **40** C2
Lake Victoria **47** D3
Lake Volta **47** C4
Lake Vyrnwy **24** D2
Lake Winnipeg **51** E3
Lambert Glacier **54**
Lambourn *river* **25** F1
Lammermuir Hills **21** G3
Lampeter **24** C2
Lanark **21** F3
Lancashire *county* **22** C2
Lancaster **22** D3
Land's End **28** B3
Langholm **21** G3
Lanzhou **42** E4
Laos **42** E3
La Paz **52** C3
Largs **20** E3
Larne **20** D2
Larne *district* **20** D2
Larsen Ice Shelf **54**
Las Vegas **50** D2
Latvia **38** D2
Launceston Australia **48** C1
Launceston UK **28** C3
Laurencekirk **19** G1
Leader Water *river* **21** G3
Lebanon **42** A4
Ledbury **25** E2
Leeds **22** D2
Leicester **25** F2
Leicester City *unitary authority* **25** F2
Leicestershire *county* **25** F2/G2
Leighton Buzzard **26** D2
Leith Hill **26** D2
Leitrim *county* **20** A2
Leominster **25** E2
Lerwick **17** D3
Lessay **29** F2
Lesser Antilles *islands* **51** F1/G1
Letchworth **26** D2
le Touquet-Paris-Plage **27** F1
Letterkenny **20** B2
Lewes **26** E1
Lewis *island* **18** C3
Leyburn **21** H2
Leyland **22** C2
Liberia **46** B4
Libreville **46** C4
Libya **46** C5/D5
Lichfield **22** D1
Liddel Water *river* **21** G3
Liechtenstein **38** C2
Lillers **27** G1
Lima **52** C3
Limavady **20** C3
Limavady *district* **20** B2/C2
Lincoln **23** E2
Lincolnshire *county* **23** E2
Lincoln Wolds *hills* **23** E2
Linlithgow **21** F3
Lisbon **38** B1
Lisburn **20** C2
Lisburn *district* **20** C2
Liskeard **28** C3
Lismore *island* **18** D1
Lithuania **38** D2
Littlehampton **29** G3
Little Minch *sound* **18** C2
Little Ouse *river* **27** E3
Liverpool **22** C2
Livingston **21** F3
Lizard **28** B2
Lizard Point **28** B2
Ljubljana **38** C2
Llandeilo **24** D1
Llandovery **24** D1
Llandrindod Wells **24** D2
Llandudno **24** D3
Llanelli **24** C1
Llangollen **24** D2
Llanidloes **24** D2
Llanos *geog. region* **53** C4
Lleyn Peninsula **24** C2/C3
Lochaline *town* **18** D1
Loch Arkaig **19** D1
Loch Awe **18/19** D1
Lochdon **18** D1
Loch Doon **21** E3
Loch Earn **19** E1
Loch Eishort **18** D2
Loch Ericht **19** E3
Loch Ericht **19** E1
Loch Etive **18/19** D1
Loch Fyne **20** D4
Lochgilphead **20** D4
Loch Katrine **21** E4
Loch Ken **21** E3
Loch Leven **21** F4
Loch Linnhe **18** D1
Loch Lochy **19** E1
Loch Lomond **21** E4
Loch Long **20/21** E4
Lochmaben *town* **21** F3
Lochmaddy *town* **18** B2
Loch Man Clar **19** E3
Loch Maree **18** D2
Loch Mullardoch **19** E2
Lochnagar *mountain* **19** F1
Loch Ness **19** E2
Loch Rannoch **19** E1
Lochranza *town* **20** D3
Loch Shiel **18** D1
Loch Shin **19** E3
Loch Snizort **18** C2
Loch Tay **19** E1
Loch Torridon **18** D2
Lockerbie **21** F3
Łódź **38** C2
Lofoten Islands **40** C3
Lomé **46** C4
London **26** D2
Londonderry **20** B2
Londonderry *district* **20** B2
Long Eaton **23** D1
Long Mynd *summit* **25** E2
Longreach **48** C2
Looe **28** C3
Lord Howe Island **49** C2
Los Angeles **50** D2
Lossiemouth **19** F2
Lostwithiel **28** C3
Lough Allen **20** A2
Lough Beg **20** C2
Loughborough **23** D1
Lough Derg **20** B2
Lough Foyle **20** B3
Lough Macnean Lower **20** B2
Lough Macnean Upper **20** B2
Lough Melvin **20** A2
Lough Neagh **20** C2
Lough Oughter **20** B2
Lough Swilly **20** B3
Louth **23** E2
Lower Lough Erne **20** B2
Lowestoft **27** F3
Lowther Hills **21** F3
Loyalty Islands **49** D2
Luanda **46** C3
Luce Bay **22** A3/B3
Ludlow **25** E2
Lundy *island* **28** C4
Lune *river* **21** G2
Lurgan **20** C2
Lusaka **46** D3
Luton **26** D2
Luton *unitary authority* **26** D2
Luxembourg **38** C2
Luzon *island* **44** F3
Lybster **19** F3
Lyme Bay **29** E3
Lyme Regis **29** E3
Lymington **29** F3
Lynton **28** D4
Lyons **38** C2
Lys *river* **27** G1
Lytham St. Anne's **22** B2

M

Mablethorpe **23** F2
Macapá **52** D4
Macclesfield **22** C2
Macdonnell Ranges *mountains* **49** B2
Macduff **19** G2
Machynlleth **24** D2
Mackenzie River **51** C4
Madagascar **46** E2/E3
Madagascar *island* **47** E2/E3
Madeira Islands **47** B5
Madras *see* Chennai
Madrid **38** B2
Magadan **43** G5
Maghera **20** C2
Magherafelt **20** C2
Magherafelt *district* **20** C2
Mahajanga **46** E3
Maidenhead **26** D2
Maidstone **27** E2
Main *river* **20** C2
Mainland Orkney Islands *island* **17** B1/B2
Mainland Shetland Islands *island* **17** D3
Majorca **40** C1
Malahide **24** A3
Malawi **46** D3
Malay Peninsula **44** E3
Malaysia **42** E3
Maldiive Archipelago *islands* **44** C3
Maldives **42** C3
Mali **46** B4
Malin Head *cape* **20** B3
Mallaig **18** D2
Malmesbury **25** E1
Malta **38** C1
Malton **23** E3
Managua **50** E1
Manaus **52** D3
Manchester **22** C2
Mangotsfield **29** E4
Manila **42** F3
Mansfield **23** D2
Maputo **46** D2
Maracaibo **52** C4
Mar del Plata **52** D2
Margate **27** F2
Marie Byrd Land **54**
Market Drayton **22** C1
Market Harborough **25** G2
Market Rasen **23** E2
Marlborough **29** F4
Marlow **26** D2
Marrakech **46** B5
Marseilles **38** C2
Marshall Islands **49** D4
Marshall Islands **48** D4
Maryport **21** F2
Maseru **46** D2
Mashhad **42** B4
Massif Central *mountains* **40** C2
Matadi **46** C3
Matlock **22** D2
Mato Grosso *admin.* **53** D3
Mauritania **46** B4/B5
Mauritius *island* **47** E2
Maybole **21** E3
Mbabane **46** D2
Medan **42** D3
Medellín **52** C4
Mediterranean Sea **40** C1/D1
Medway *river* **27** E2
Medway *unitary authority* **27** E2
Meig *river* **19** E2
Mekong River **44** E3
Melbourne **48** C2
Melton Mowbray **23** E1
Memphis **50** E2
Mendip Hills **29** E4
Mendoza **52** C2
Meon *river* **29** F3
Mere **29** E4
Mersey *river* **22** C2
Merseyside *county* **22** C2
Merthyr Tydfil **24** D1
Merthyr Tydfil *unitary authority* **24** D1
Merton **26** D2
Meseta **40** B1/B2
Mexico **50** E1
México **50** D2/E1
Miami **50** E2
Mickle Fell *mountain* **21** G2
Micronesia **48** C2
Middlesborough **23** D3
Middlesborough *unitary authority* **23** D3
Midlothian *unitary authority* **21** F3
Milan **38** C2
Mildenhall **27** E3
Milford Haven **24** B1
Milton Keynes **26** D3
Milton Keynes *unitary authority* **26** D3
Milton Ness *cape* **19** G1
Milwaukee **50** E3
Mindanao *island* **44** F3
Mindoro *island* **44** F3
Minehead **28** D4
Mingulay *island* **18** B1
Minneapolis **50** E3
Minorca **40** C1
Minsk **38** D2
Mississippi River **51** E2
Missouri River **51** D3
Moçambique **46** E3
Moffat **21** F3
Mogadishu **46** E4
Mold **24** D3
Moldova **38** D2
Mombasa **46** D3
Monadhliath Mountains **19** E2
Monaghan **20** C2
Monaghan *county* **20** B2/C2
Mongolia **42** E5
Monmouth **25** E1
Monmouthshire *unitary authority* **25** E1
Monrovia **46** B4
Mont Blanc *mountain* **40** C2
Monterrey **50** D2
Montevideo **52** D2
Montgomery **24** D2
Montréal **50** F3
Montrose **19** G1
Moray *unitary authority* **19** F2
Moray Firth *estuary* **19** F2
Morecambe **22** D3
Morecambe Bay **22** D3
Moreton-in-Marsh **25** F1
Morocco **46** B5
Morven *mountain* **19** F3
Moscow **38** D2
Motherwell **21** E3
Mount Aconcagua **53** C2
Mount Ararat **44** B4
Mount Cameroon *mountain* **47** C4
Mount Cook **49** D1
Mount Demavend **44** B4
Mount Elbrus **41** E2
Mount Erebus **54**
Mount Etna **40** C1
Mount Everest **44** D4

Mount Forel **55**
Mount Hekla **40** B3
Mount Isa *town* **48** B2
Mount Kenya **47** D3
Mount Kilimanjaro **47** D3
Mount Kinabalu **44** E3
Mount Kirkpatrick **54**
Mount Kosciusko **49** C2
Mount Logan **51** B4
Mount McKinley **51** A4
Mount Markham **54**
Mount Meharry **49** A2
Mount Menzies **54**
Mount Olympus **40** D2
Mounts Bay **28** B3
Mount Stanley **47** D4
Mount Whitney **51** D2
Mount Wilhelm **49** C3
Mouths of the Ganges **44** D4
Moyle *district* **20** C3
Mozambique **46** D2/D3
Mozambique Channel **47** D2/E3
Muck *island* **18** C1
Muckle Roe *island* **17** D3
Mull *island* **18** C1/D1
Mull Head *cape* **17** C2
Mullion **28** B3
Mull of Galloway **21** E2
Mull of Kintyre **20** D3
Mull of Oa **20** C3
Mumbai **42** C3
Munich **38** C2
Murmansk **38** D3
Murray River **49** C2
Muscat **42** B4
Musselburgh **21** F3
Myanmar (Burma) **42** D3
Mynydd Eppynt *hills* **24** D2
Mynydd Preseli *hills* **24** C1

N

Nagoya **42** F4
Nairn **19** F2
Nairn *river* **19** E2
Nairobi **46** D3
Namib Desert **47** C2
Namibia **46** C2/C3
Nanchang **42** E4
Nanjing **42** E4
Nantes **38** B2
Naples **38** C2
Narvik **38** C3
Nassau **50** F2
Natal **52** E3
Nauru **48** D3
Nauru *island* **49** D3
Ndjamena **46** C4
Neath **24** D1
Neath Port Talbot *unitary authority* **24** D1
Nelson New Zealand **48** D1
Nelson UK **22** C2
Nelson River **51** E3
Nene *river* **27** E3
Nepal **42** D4
Netherlands **38** C2
Netherlands Antilles *islands* **52** C4
Newark-on-Trent **23** E2
Newburgh **19** F1
Newbury **29** F4
New Caledonia *island* **49** D2
Newcastle Australia **48** C2
Newcastle UK **20** D2
Newcastle Emlyn **24** C2
Newcastle-under-Lyme **22** C2
Newcastle upon Tyne **21** H2
New Cumnock **21** E3
Newfoundland *island* **51** G3
New Galloway **21** E3
New Guinea *island* **44** F2/G2
Newmarket **27** E3
New Orleans **50** E2
New Plymouth **48** D2
Newport Isle of Wight **29** F3
Newport Shropshire **22** C1
Newport Wales **24** D1
Newport *unitary authority* **24** D1/E1
Newquay **28** B3
New Quay **24** C2
Newry **20** C2
Newry and Mourne *district* **20** C2
New Siberian Islands **55**
Newton Abbot **28** D3
Newton Aycliffe **21** H2
Newtonmore **19** E2
Newton Stewart **21** E2
Newtown **24** D2
Newtownabbey **20** D2
Newtownabbey *district* **20** D2
Newtownards **20** D2
Newtownhamilton **20** C2
Newtownstewart **20** B2
New York **50** F3
New Zealand **48** D1/D2
Niagara Falls **51** F3
Niamey **46** C4
Nicaragua **50** E1
Nicobar Islands **44** D3
Nicosia **38** D1
Nidd *river* **22** D3
Nieuwpoort **27** G2
Niger **46** C4
Niger Delta **47** C4
Nigeria **46** C4
Nile Delta **47** D5
Nile River **47** D5
Nith *river* **21** F3
Nizhniy Novgorod **39** E2
Norfolk **50** F2
Norfolk *county* **27** E3/F3
Norfolk Broads **27** F3
Norfolk Island **49** D2
Northallerton **23** D3
Northampton **26** D3
Northamptonshire *county* **26** C3/D3
North Ayrshire *unitary authority* **20/21** D3/E3
North Cape **40** D3
North Channel **20** D2/D3
North Down *district* **20** D2
North Downs *hills* **27** E2
North Dvina River **41** E3
North East Lincolnshire *unitary authority* **23** E2
Northern Ireland **12**
North Esk *river* **19** G1
North European Plain **40** C2/D2
North Foreland *cape* **27** F2
North Island **49** D2
North Korea **42** F4
North Lanarkshire *unitary authority* **21** F3
North Lincolnshire *unitary authority* **23** E2
North Ronaldsay *island* **17** C2
North Saskatchewan River **51** D3
North Sea **40** C2
North Shields **23** D4
North Somerset *unitary authority* **26** B2
North Uist *island* **18** B2
Northumberland *county* **21** G3/H3
Northwest Highlands **18/19** D2/E3
Northwich **22** C2
North York Moors **23** E3
North Yorkshire *county* **22/23** D3
Norton **23** E3
Norway **38** B2/C3
Norwich **27** F3
Nottingham **23** D1
Nottingham City *unitary authority* **23** D1
Nottinghamshire *county* **23** D2/E2
Nouakchott **46** B4
Noumea **48** D2
Nova Iguaçu **52** D2
Novaya Zemlya *islands* **55**
Novosibirsk **42** D5
Nullarbor Plain **49** B2
Nuneaton **25** F2
Nuuk **55**

O

Oban **18** D1
Ochil Hills **21** F4
Odessa **38** D2
Oiapoque **52** D4
Ojos del Salado *mountain* **53** C2
Okavango Swamp **47** D2/D3
Okehampton **28** C3
Oldham **22** C2
Oldmeldrum **19** G2
Omagh **20** B2
Omagh *district* **20** B2
Oman **42** B4
Omsk **42** C5
Oostende **27** G2
Oporto **38** B2
Orford Ness *cape* **27** F3
Orkney Isles *unitary authority* **17** B1/C2
Orne *river* **29** G2
Oronsay *island* **20** C4
Osaka **42** F4
Oslo **38** C2
Oswestry **22** B1
Ottawa **50** F3
Ouagadougou **46** B4
Oundle **26** D3
Ouse *river* **23** E2
Outer Hebrides *islands* **18** B1/C3
Out Skerries *islands* **17** E3
Oxford **25** F1
Oxfordshire *county* **25** F1

P

Pabbay *island* **18** B2
Pacific Ocean **44** G4/J4
Padstow **28** C3
Paisley **21** E3
Pakistan **42** C4
Palembang **42** E2
Palermo **38** C1
Pampa *geog. region* **53** C2/D2
Panamá **50** F1
Panama **50** E1
Papa Stour *island* **17** D3
Papa Westray *island* **17** C2
Papua New Guinea **48** C3
Paraguay **52** C2/D2
Paramaribo **52** D4
Paris **38** C2
Parrett *river* **29** E4
Patagonia *geog. region* **53** C1/C2
Peace River **51** C3/D3
Peebles **21** F3
Peel **21** E2
Peel Fell *summit* **21** G3
Peloponnese *island* **40** D1
Pembrokshire *unitary authority* **24** B1/C1
Penicuik **21** F3
Pennines *hills* **21** G2
Penrith **21** G2
Penryn **28** B3
Pentland Firth *sound* **17** B1
Pentland Hills **21** F3
Pen-y-ghent *summit* **21** G2
Penzance **28** B3
Perm **39** E2
Perth Australia **48** A2
Perth UK **19** F1
Perth and Kinross *unitary authority* **19** E1/F1
Peru **52** C3
Peterborough **26** D3
Peterborough *unitary authority* **26** D3
Peterhead **19** H2
Peterlee **23** D3
Petersfield **26** D2
Philadelphia **50** F3
Philippines **42** E3/F3
Phnom Penh **42** E3
Phoenix **50** D2
Phoenix Islands **49** E3
Pickering **23** E3
Pitlochry **19** F1
Pittsburgh **50** F3
Plymouth **28** C3
Plymouth *unitary authority* **28** C3
Plynlimon *mountain* **24** D2
Pointe-Noire *town* **46** C3
Point of Fethaland **17** D3
Poland **38** C2/D2
Pontardulais **24** C1
Pontefract **23** D2
Pontypool **24** D1
Pontypridd **24** D1
Poole **29** F3
Poole *unitary authority* **29** F3
Poolewe **18** D2
Popocatepetl *volcano* **51** E1
Portadown **20** C2
Port Askaig **20** C3
Port Augusta **48** B2
Port-au-Prince **50** F1
Port Elizabeth **46** D2
Port Ellen **20** C3
Port Glasgow **21** E3
Port Harcourt **46** C4
Porthmadog **24** C2
Portknockie **19** G2
Portland **50** C3
Portland Bill *cape* **29** E3
Port Moresby **48** C3
Portnahaven **20** C3
Pôrto Alegre **52** D2
Port of Ness **18** C3
Porto Novo **46** C4
Pôrto Velho **52** C3
Portpatrick **20** D2
Portree **18** C2
Portrush **20** C3
Portsmouth **29** F3
Portsmouth *unitary authority* **29** F3
Portsoy **19** G2
Portstewart **20** C3
Port Sudan **46** D4
Port Talbot **24** D1
Portugal **38** B1/B2
Powys *unitary authority* **24** D2
Poznań **38** C2
Prague **38** C2
Preston **22** C2
Prestwick **21** E3
Pretoria **46** D2
Prince Rupert **50** C3
Príncipe *island* **47** C4
Pripet Marshes **40** D2
Pucallpa **52** C3
Puebla **50** E1
Puerto Montt **52** C1
Puerto Rico **50** F1
Punta Arenas **52** C1
Pusan **42** F4
Pwllheli **24** C2
Pyongyang **42** F4
Pyrenees *mountains* **40** B2/C2

Q

Qatar **42** B4
Qattara Depression **47** C5/D5
Qingdao **42** F4
Quantock Hills **29** D4
Québec **50** F3
Queen Maud Land **54**
Quezon **42** F3
Quito **52** C3

R

Raasay *island* **18** C2
Rabat-Salé **46** B5
Ramsey **21** E2
Ramsgate **27** F2
Randalstown **20** C2
Rangoon **42** D3
Rathlin Island **20** C3
Rathlin Sound **20** C3
Rattray **19** F1
Reading **26** D2
Reading *unitary authority* **26** C2/D2
Recife **52** E3
Red Basin **44** E4
Redbridge **27** E2
Redcar **23** D3
Redcar and Cleveland *unitary authority* **23** D3/E3
Redditch **25** F2
Rede *river* **21** G3
Redhill *town* **26** D2
Redruth **28** B3
Red Sea **47** D5
Regina **50** D3
Reigate **26** D2
Renfrewshire *unitary authority* **21** E3
Republic of Ireland **38** B2
Republic of South Africa **46** C2/D2
Réunion *island* **47** E2
Reykjavík **38** A3
Rhayader **24** D2
Rhondda **24** D1
Rhondda Cynon Taff *unitary authority* **24** D1
Rhum *island* **18** C1/C2
Rhyl **24** D3
Ribble *river* **22** C2
Richmond **21** H2
Richmond upon Thames **26** D2
Riga **38** D2
Ringwood **29** F3
Rio de Janeiro *town* **52** D2
Río Grande *river* **51** D2
Ripon **21** H2
River Amazon **53** C3/D3
River Amur **44** F5
River Congo **47** D4
River Danube **40** D2
River Dnieper **40** D2
River Dniester **40** D2
River Duero **40** B2
River Ebro **40** B2
River Elbe **40** C2
River Euphrates **44** B4
River Ganges **44** D4
River Glomma **40** C3
River Indus **44** C4
River Irtysh **44** C5
River Kolyma **45** G6
River Lena **44** F6
River Loire **40** C2
River Madeira **53** C3
River Niger **47** B4
River Ob **44** C6
River Orange **47** C2/D2
River Orinoco **53** C4
River Paraguay **53** D2/D3
River Paraná **53** C2/D2
River Plate *estuary* **53** D2
River Po **40** C2
River Rhine **40** C2
River Rhône **40** C2
River Seine **40** C2
River Swilly **20** B3
River Tagus **40** B1
River Thames **40** B2
River Tigris **44** B4
River Tocantins **53** D3
River Ural **41** E2
River Vaal **47** D2
River Vistula **40** C2/D2
River Volga **41** E2
Riyadh **42** B4
Rochdale **22** C2
Rochester **27** E2
Rockhampton **48** C2
Rocky Mountains **51** C4/D2
Romania **38** D2
Rome **38** C2
Romsey **29** F3
Ronne Ice Shelf **54**
Rora Head **17** B1
Rosario **52** C2
Rosehearty **19** G2
Ross Ice Shelf **54**
Ross of Mull *bay* **20** C1
Ross-on-Wye **25** E1
Ross Sea **54**
Rostov-on-Don **39** D2
Rotherham **23** D2
Rothes **19** F2
Rothesay **20** D3
Rotterdam **38** C2
Rousay *island* **17** B2
Royal Leamington Spa **25** F2
Royal Tunbridge Wells **27** E2
Royston **26** D3
Rubha Hunish *cape* **18** C2
Rugby **25** F2
Rugeley **22** D1
Runcorn **22** C2
Russian Federation (Russia) **42** A5/F5
Rutland *unitary authority* **23** E1
Rutland Water **23** E1
Rwanda **46** D3
Rybinsk Reservoir **40/41** D2
Ryde **29** F3
Rye **27** E1
Ryukyu Islands **44** F4

S

Sacramento **50** C2
Saffron Walden **27** E3
Sahara Desert **47** B5/D5
St. Abb's Head *cape* **21** G3
St. Agnes **28** B3
St. Albans **26** D2
St. Albans Head *cape* **29** E3
St. Andrews **19** G1
St. Austell **28** C3
St. Bees Head **21** F2
St. Bride's Bay **24** B1
St. Catherine's Point *cape* **29** F3
St. David's **24** B1
St. David's Head **24** B1
St. George's Channel **24** A1/B2
St. Helens **22** C2
St. Helier **29** E2
St. Ives Cambridgeshire **26** D3
St. Ives Cornwall **28** B3
St. John's **50** G3
St. John's Point **20** D2
St. John's Town of Dalry **21** E3
St. Just **28** B3
St. Kitts-Nevis **50** F1
St. Lawrence River **51** F3
St.-Lô **29** F2
St. Louis **50** E2
St. Lucia **50** F1
St. Magnus Bay **17** D3
St. Mary's *island* **28** A2
St. Mary's Loch **21** F3
St. Neots **26** D3
St.-Omer **27** G1
St. Peter Port **29** E2
St. Petersburg **38** D2
Saint-Pierre and Miquelon *islands* **50** G3
St. Vincent and the Grenadines **50** F1
Salcombe **28** D3
Sale **22** C2
Salford **22** C2
Salisbury **29** F4
Salisbury Plain **29** F4
Salta **52** C2
Saltash **28** C3
Saltcoats **21** E3
Salt Lake City **50** D3
Salvador **52** E3
Salween River **44** D3/D4
Samara **42** B5
Samoa **48** E3
Samoa Islands **49** E3
San'a **42** B3
San Antonio **50** E2
Sanday *island* **17** C2
San Diego **50** D2
Sandown **29** F3
San Francisco **50** C2
San José **50** E1
San Juan **50** F1
Sanquhar **21** F3
San Salvador **50** E1
Santa Cruz **52** C3
Santa Cruz Islands **49** D3
Santa Marta **52** C4
Santarém **52** D3
Santiago **52** C2
Santo Domingo **50** F1
São Francisco *river* **53** D3
São Luís **52** D3
São Paulo **52** D2
São Tomé *island* **47** C4
São Tomé and Príncipe **46** C3/C4
Sapporo **42** G5
Sarajevo **38** C2
Sardinia **40** C2
Sark *island* **29** E2
Saudi Arabia **42** B4
Sawel *mountain* **20** B2
Scalasaig **20** C4
Scalloway **17** D3
Scalpay **18** C2/D2
Scandinavian Highlands **40** C3/D3
Scapa **17** C1
Scapa Flow *sound* **17** B1
Scarba *island* **20** D4

Scarborough **23** E3
Scarp *island* **18** B3
Scotland **12**
Scottish Borders *unitary authority* **21** F3/G3
Scunthorpe **23** E2
Sea of Azov **40/41** D2
Sea of Japan **44** F4/F5
Sea of Okhotsk **44/45** G5
Seascale **21** F2
Seaton **29** D3
Seattle **50** C3
Selby **23** D2
Selkirk **21** G3
Selsey Bill **29** G3
Selvas **53** C3
Semarang **42** E2
Senegal **46** B4
Senegal River **47** B4
Sennen **28** B3
Seoul **42** F4
Sevenoaks **27** E2
Severn *river* **25** E1
Severnaya Zemlya *islands* **55**
Seville **38** B1
Seychelles *islands* **47** E3
Sgurr Mór *mountain* **19** D2
Shaftesbury **29** E4
Shanghai **42** F4
Shanklin **29** F3
Shannon *river* **20** B2
Shapinsay *island* **17** C2
Sheerness **27** E2
Sheffield **23** D2
Shenyang **42** F5
Shepton Mallet **29** E4
Sherborne **29** E3
Sheringham **27** F3
Shetland Islands *unitary authority* **17** D3
Shiant Islands **18** C2
Shiel *river* **18** D2
Shikoku *island* **44** F4
Shrewsbury **22** C1
Shropshire *county* **25** E2
Siberian Lowland **44** C6/D6
Sicily **40** C1
Sidlaw Hills **19** F1/G1
Sidmouth **29** D3
Sierra Leone **46** B4
Sierra Madre *mountains* **51** D2
Sierra Nevada *mountains* **51** C2/C3
Simpson Desert **49** B2
Singapore **42** E3
Skegness **23** F2
Skelmersdale **22** C2
Skiddaw *mountain* **21** F2
Skipton **22** C2
Skopje **38** D2
Skye *island* **18** C2
Slave River **51** D3/D4
Sleaford **23** E1
Slieve Donard *mountain* **20** D2
Slieve Snaght *summit* **20** B3
Slough **26** D2
Slough *unitary authority* **26** D2
Slovakia **38** C2/D2
Slovenia **38** C2
Snaefell *mountain* **21** E2
Snake River **51** D3
Snowdon *mountain* **24** C3
Soar *river* **26** C3
Soay *island* **18** C2
Socotra *island* **44** B3
Sofiya **38** D2
Solihull **25** F2
Solomon Islands **49** C3/D3
Solomon Islands **48** C3/D3
Solway Firth **21** F2
Somalia **46** E4
Somerset *county* **29** D4/E4
Sound of Arisaig **18** D1
Sound of Bute **20** D3
Sound of Harris **18** B2
Sound of Jura **20** D3/D4
Sound of Mull **18** D1
Sound of Sleat **18** D2
Southampton **29** F3
Southampton *unitary authority* **29** F3
South Ayrshire *unitary authority* **20/21** D2/E3
South Barrule *hill* **21** E2
South Benfleet **27** E2
South China Sea **44** E3
South Downs *hills* **26** D1
Southend **20** D3
Southend *unitary authority* **27** E2
Southend-on-Sea **27** E2
Southern Ocean **54**
Southern Uplands **21** E3/G3
South Esk *river* **19** G1
South Georgia *island* **53** E1
South Island **49** D1
South Gloucestershire *unitary authority* **26** B2
South Korea **42** F4
South Lanarkshire *unitary authority* **21** E3/F
South Molton **28** D4
South Orkney Islands **54**
South Pole **54**
Southport **22** B2
South Ronaldsay *island* **17** C1
South Saskatchewan River **51** D3
South Shetland Islands **54**
South Shields **21** H3
South Uist *island* **18** B2
Southwold **27** F3
South Yorkshire *county* **22/23** D2
Spain **38** B1/C2
Spennymoor *town* **21** H2
Spey *river* **19** F2
Spilsby **23** F2
Spurn Head *cape* **23** F2
Sri Lanka **42** C3
Stafford **22** C1
Staffordshire *county* **22** C1/D1
Staines **26** D2
Stamford **26** D3
Stanley **52** D1
Start Bay **28** D3
Start Point *cape* **28** D3
Stavanger **38** C2
Stevenage **26** D2
Stewart Island **49** D1
Stinchar *river* **21** E3
Stirling **21** F4
Stirling *unitary authority* **21** E4
Stockbridge **29** F4
Stockholm **38** C2
Stockport **22** C2
Stockton-on-Tees **23** D3
Stockton-on-Tees *unitary authority* **23** D3
Stoke-on-Trent **22** C2
Stoke-on-Trent *unitary authority* **22** C1/C2
Stonehaven **19** G1
Stornoway **18** C3
Stour Dorset *river* **29** E3
Stour Suffolk *river* **27** E3
Stourbridge **25** E2
Stourport-on-Severn **25** E2
Stowmarket **27** F3
Stow-on-the-Wold **25** F1
Strabane **20** B2
Strabane *district* **20** B2
Strait of Dover **27** F1/F2
Strait of Gibraltar **40** B1
Strangford Lough **20** D2
Stranraer **20** D2
Stratford-upon-Avon **25** F2
Strathy Point **19** E3
Stromness **17** B1
Stronsay *island* **17** C2
Stronsay Firth *sound* **17** C2
Stroud **25** E1
Strumble Head **24** B2
Sturt Desert **49** C2
Sucre **52** C3
Sudan **46** D4
Sudbury Canada **50** E3
Sudbury UK **27** E3
Suez **46** D5
Suffolk *county* **27** E3/F3
Sulawesi *island* **44** E2/F2
Sumatra *island* **44** D3/E2
Sumburgh Head *cape* **17** D2
Sunderland **21** H2
Surabaya **42** E2
Suriname **52** D4
Surrey *county* **26** D2
Sutton **26** D2
Sutton Coldfield **25** F2
Sutton in Ashfield **23** D2
Suva **48** D3
Swaffham **27** E3
Swale *river* **21** H2
Swanage **29** F3
Swansea **24** D1
Swansea *unitary authority* **24** C1
Swaziland **46** D2
Sweden **38** C2/D3
Swindon **25** F1
Swindon *unitary authority* **25** F2
Switzerland **38** C2
Swords **24** A3
Sydney Australia **48** C2
Sydney Canada **50** F3
Symbister **17** D3
Syria **42** A4

T

Tabriz **42** B4
Tadcaster **23** D2
Tain **19** E2
Taipei **42** F4
Taiwan **42** F4
Taiyuan **42** E4
Tajikistan **42** C4
Tallinn **38** D2
Tamar *river* **28** C3
Tampa **50** E2
Tamworth **25** E2
Tanzania **46** D3
Taransay *island* **18** B2
Tarbat Ness **19** F2
Tarbert Strathclyde **20** D3
Tarbert Western Isles **18** C2
Tarbet **21** E4
Tashkent **42** C5
Tasmania *island* **49** C1
Tasman Sea **49** C2/D2
Taunton **29** D4
Taurus Mountains **40/41** D1
Tavistock **28** C3
Tavy *river* **28** C3
Taw *river* **28** D3
Tay *river* **19** F1
Tbilişi **39** E2
Tees *river* **21** G2
Tegucigalpa **50** E1
Tehran **42** B4
Teifi *river* **24** C2
Teign *river* **28** D3
Teignmouth **28** D3
Telford **22** C1
Telford and Wrekin *unitary authority* **22** C1
Teme *river* **25** E2
Tenby **24** C1
Tennant Creek *town* **48** B3
Teresina **52** D3
Test *river* **29** F4
Tétouan **46** B5
Teviot *river* **21** G3
Tewkesbury **25** E1
Thailand **42** E3
Thame *river* **26** D2
Thames *river* **27** E2
Thar Desert **44** C4
The Bahamas **50** F2
The Deeps *bay* **17** D3
The Fens *region* **23** E1/F1
The Gambia **46** B4
The Great Lakes **51** E3
The Gulf **44** B4
The Minch *sound* **18** C3/D3
The Needles *rocks* **29** F3
The Peak *mountain* **22** D2
The Solent *sound* **29** F3
The Storr *mountain* **18** C2
Thessaloníka **38** D2
Thetford **27** E3
The Vale of Glamorgan *unitary authority* **24** D1
The Wash *bay* **27** E3
The Weald *geog. region* **27** E2
The Wrekin *peak* **22** C1
Thimphu **42** D4
Thirsk **23** D3
Thornaby-on-Tees **23** D3
Thornhill **21** F3
Thurrock *unitary authority* **27** E2
Thurso **19** F3
Thurso *river* **19** F3
Tianjin **42** E4
Tibetan Plateau **44** D4
Tierra del Fuego *island* **53** C1
Tignabruaich **20** D3
Timor Sea **44** F2
Tiranë **38** C2
Tiree *island* **18** C1
Titograd **38** C2
Tiverton **28** D3
Toamasina **46** E3
Tobermory **18** C1
Togo **46** C4
Tokyo **42** F4
Toliara **46** E2
Tonbridge **27** E2
Tonga **48** E2
Tonga Islands **49** E2
Torbay **28** D3
Torbay *unitary authority* **28** D3
Torfean *unitary authority* **24** D1
Toronto **50** F3
Torpoint *town* **28** C3
Torridge *river* **28** C3
Tory Island **20** A3
Tory Sound **20** A3
Totnes **28** D3
Towcester **26** D3
Townsville **48** C3
Trent *river* **23** E2
Tresco *island* **28** A2
Trevose Head *cape* **28** B3
Trinidad and Tobago **50** F1
Tripoli **46** C5
Trondheim **38** C3
Troon **21** E3
Trowbridge **29** E4
Truro **28** B3
Tucson **50** D2
Tunis **46** C5
Tunisia **46** C5
Turin **38** C2
Turkey **38** D1/D2
Turkmenistan **42** B4
Turriff **19** G2
Tweed *river* **21** F3
Tyndrum **19** E1
Tyne *river* **22** D3
Tyne and Wear *county* **23** D3/D4
Tynemouth **23** D4
Tyrrhenien Sea **40** C1/C2
Tywi *river* **24** C1

U

Uberaba **52** D3
Ufa **42** B5
Uganda **46** D4
Ukraine **38** D2
Ulan Bator **42** E5
Ullapool **18** D2
Ullswater *lake* **21** G2
Ulva *island* **18** C1
United Arab Emirates (U.A.E.) **42** B4
United Kingdom (UK) **38** B2
United States of America (USA) **50** C2/F2
Unst *island* **17** E3
Upper Lough Erne *lake* **20** B2
Ural Mountains **44** B5/C6
Ure *river* **21** H2
Uruguay **52** D2
Usk **24** D1
Uttoxeter **22** D1
Uzbekistan **42** C4/C5

V

Valdés Peninsula **53** C1
Valencia Spain **38** B1
Valencia Venezuela **52** C4
Vale of Pickering **23** E3
Vale of York **23** D3
Valognes **29** F2
Valparaíso **52** C2
Vancouver **50** C3
Vancouver Island **51** C3
Vanuatu **48** D3
Venezuela **52** C4
Veurne **27** G2
Victoria Falls **47** D3
Victoria Island **51** D4
Vienna **38** C2
Vientiane **42** E3
Vietnam **42** E3
Vila **48** D3
Vilnius **38** D2
Vinson Massif *mountains* **54**
Vire *river* **29** F2
Vitória **52** D2
Volgograd **39** E2
Vyrnwy *river* **24** D2

W

Wadebridge **28** C3
Wakefield **23** D2
Walbury Hill **29** F4
Wales **12**
Wallasey **22** B2
Walls **17** D3
Walsall **25** E2
Waltham Forest **26** D2
Walton on the Naze **27** F2
Walvis Bay *town* **46** C2
Wansbeck *river* **21** H3
Wantage **25** F1
Ward Hill **17** B1
Ward's Stone *hill* **22** D3
Wareham **29** E3
Warley **25** F2
Warminster **29** E4
Warrenpoint *town* **20** C2
Warrington **22** C2
Warrington *unitary authority* **22** C2
Warsaw **38** D2
Warwick **25** F2
Warwickshire *county* **25** F2
Washington **21** H2
Washington D.C. **50** F2
Waterlooville **29** F3
Water of Luce **20/21** E2
Watford **26** D2
Waveney *river* **27** F3
Wear *river* **21** G2
Weddell Sea **54**
Welland *river* **26** D3
Wellingborough **26** D3
Wellington New Zealand **48** D1
Wellington UK **29** D3
Wells **29** E4
Wells-next-the-Sea **27** E3
Welshpool **24** D2
Welwyn Garden City **26** D2
Wenlock Edge *hills* **25** E2
Wenzhou **42** F4
West Berkshire *unitary authority* **26** C2
West Bromwich **25** F2
Westbury **29** E4
West Dunbartonshire *unitary authority* **21** E3/E4
Western Ghats *mountains* **44** C3
Western Isles *unitary authority* **18** C3
Western Sahara **46** B5
West Indies *islands* **51** F2/G1
West Lothian *unitary authority* **21** F3
West Midlands *county* **25** E2/F2
Weston-super-Mare **29** E4
Westray *island* **17** B2/C2
Westray Firth *sound* **17** B2/C2
West Sussex *county* **26** D1
West Yorkshire *county* **22/23** D2
Wetherby **23** D2
Weymouth **29** E3
Whalsay *island* **17** E3
Wharfe *river* **23** D2
Whernside *summit* **21** G2
Whitby **23** E3
Whitchurch **22** C1
Whiteadder Water *river* **21** G3
Whitehaven **21** F2
White Sea **40** D3
Whithorn **21** E2
Whitley Bay *town* **21** H3
Wick **19** F3
Wicklow **24** A2
Widnes **22** C2
Wigan **22** C2
Wigston **23** D1
Wigton **21** F2
Wigtown **21** E2
Wigtown Bay **21** E1
Wilkes Land **54**
Wiltshire *county* **29** E4/F4
Wimborne Minster **29** F3
Wincanton **29** E4
Winchester **29** F4
Windermere **21** G2
Windermere *lake* **21** G2
Windhoek **46** C2
Windsor **26** D2
Windsor and Maidenhead *unitary authority* **26** D2
Winnipeg **50** E3
Winsford **22** C2
Wisbech **27** E3
Wishaw **21** F3
Witham **27** E2
Witham *river* **23** E2
Witney **25** F1
Woking **26** D2
Wokingham **26** D2
Wokingham *unitary authority* **26** C2/D2
Wolverhampton **25** E2
Woodbridge **27** F3
Wooler **21** G3
Worcester **25** E2
Worcestershire *county* **25** E2
Workington **21** F2
Worksop **23** D2
Worms Head *cape* **24** C1
Worthing **29** G3
Wrexham **22** C2
Wrexham *unitary authority* **24** D3
Wuhan **42** E4
Wye *river* **24** D2
Wymondham **27** F3
Wyndham **48** B3
Wyre *river* **22** C2

X

Xi'an **42** E4

Y

Yakutsk **42** F6
Yamoussoukro **46** B4
Yangtze River **44** E4
Yaoundé **46** C4
Yap Islands **49** B4
Yarrow Water *river* **21** F3
Yekaterinburg **42** C5
Yell *island* **17** D3
Yellowknife **50** D4
Yellow Sea **44** F4
Yell Sound **17** D3
Yemen Republic **42** B3
Yenisey River **44** D6
Yeo *river* **29** E4
Yeovil **29** E3
Yerevan **42** B5
Yes Tor *summit* **28** C3
Yingkou **42** F5
Yokohama **42** F4
York **23** D2
York *unitary authority* **23** D2
Yorkshire Wolds *hills* **23** E3
Yucatan Peninsula **51** E1/E2
Yugoslavia **38** C2/D2
Yukon River **51** A4

Z

Zagreb **38** C2
Zagros Mountains **44** B4
Zambezi River **47** D3
Zambia **46** D3
Zibo **42** E4
Zimbabwe **46** D2/D3